SWEET GREEK™

SWEET GREEK™

SIMPLE FOOD & SUMPTUOUS FEASTS

KATHY TSAPLES

MELBOURNE BOOKS

Dedication

My beautiful father was an intelligent man who
never had the chance to receive a formal education.
But this did not stop him from reading — he read
book after book of whatever would interest him.
In his final days he was reading *Zorba the Greek*
by Nikos Kazantzakis. Whenever I would ask him how
he was, he would reply, 'I am in a hurry to finish
the book before I die.'

Sadly, when he passed away he had only one more
chapter to go. I read this to him at his grave.
Now you have finished the book, Dad.

Nikos Kazantzakis, in *Zorba the Greek*,
wrote the following:

'I at last realised that eating was a spiritual
function and that meat, bread and wine were
the raw materials from which the mind is made.'

For you, Dad.

Cook's Note

Taste, taste and taste again.

Greek cuisine—especially traditional home cooking—is simple, using only a few of the best ingredients. It is not measurement-and precision-driven. The exceptions, of course, are the sweets. Also remember that, taking your time and cooking things slowly always gives a better result, allowing the flavours to fully develop.

My recipes serve between four to six people. I have tried to provide as accurate a measure as possible, but when it comes to olive oil, lemon juice, salt, pepper and herbs (both fresh and dried) you can add as little or as much as you like according to your taste. Where the recipe calls for it to be tangy, I have noted this.

Always use the best extra virgin olive oil unless you are frying, in which case use sunflower oil.

When cooking lamb, I prefer the Salt Bush variety. By the same token, always use organic free-range pork.

Whenever I am roasting I use the fan-forced mode. If you don't have fan-forced, add another 20°C to the temperature I have indicated.

Take these recipes, cook them, embrace them and make them your own. Create your own family celebration and memories

... and don't forget to drizzle some additional olive oil over all your finished dishes. It is the best way to finish off a dish!

INTRODUCTION

Australia, the promised land. The place where dreams come true. My mother and father were two people among the many thousands that migrated to this country with a dream for a better life. They arrived with only a suitcase, no money and no language skills, leaving behind their families and a country that was poverty-stricken and devoid of any opportunities for growth and development.

Both my parents are from an area called Thessaly, considered to be the great plain of Greece. It is an important agricultural area, particularly for the production of grain, cattle and sheep. For as far as the eye can see, there are cotton, wheat and corn fields. It's also renowned for its cheese production. Many of Greece's traditional dishes, especially pies — for example, Spanakopita and Prasopita (made with leeks and cheese) — contain cheese, thus placing Thessaly at the core of Greece's pita (pie) culture.

The capital of Thessaly is Larisa. Larisa has a Mediterranean climate, with hot summers and cold winters, and in the vicinity of Mount Olympus the winter is harsh. My mother's village, called Karya, is located at the foothills of the south side of Mount Olympus. Despite being a small village it has a rich tradition, both mythological and folk (Mount Olympus is the mountain home of the Greek gods). My mother was the youngest of four girls, but without a doubt the most gutsy and determined. As a child, she trained to become a professional dressmaker, following in the footsteps of her father, who was a tailor. This is how her family made a living. My mother, her eldest sister Katina, and my grandfather sewed while their other sister Effie did all the manual work, ploughing in the fields and so on. They were difficult years, as we were told over and over again. Poverty-stricken and affected by the First and Second World Wars and a civil war, they experienced the burning of homes in their village. My mother's family home was destroyed by the Germans, which meant that, after the war, the girls had to carry one stone after another until the house was built again. Such strength, determination and, above all, courage.

My father was the eldest of seven children. He left the Gonnous region of Thessaly, where his family lived, and arrived in Australian in 1955 on a ship called *Tasmania*, settling in Fitzroy to begin with. The following year, my mother, then only nineteen years of age, crossed the seas on the same ship; this was to be its last journey. From 1953 until June 1956, over 33,000 Greek migrants arrived in Australia. A significant number of them were destined for Bonegilla, and my father was one of them.

It is extraordinary to imagine that it was only sixty years ago that the Australian government established an agreement with the Greek government, opening a pathway for Greeks to migrate to the 'Lucky Country'. It was the 1952 'Assisted Passage' agreement that had the most impact, enabling Victoria to become the third-largest Greek state outside Athens and Thessaloniki.

It was in these
houses and in the
factories they
worked in that
the first exchanges
of recipes from
the homeland began.
The foundations
of traditional
Greek cuisine
as we know it
in Australia
had been formed.

My parents were eventually introduced to each other and,
in January 1956, married at the Evangelismo Greek Orthodox
Church on Victoria Parade, East Melbourne. One of the dearest
and yet saddest stories my mother has shared with me is how,
despite her young age, she had to prepare the food for the
wedding party, get dressed and then walk to Evangelismo all
by herself. There was no one to help her, nurture her or
escort her to the church. In the beginning, my parents shared
houses with many different couples to save money. It was
in these houses and in the factories they worked in that
the first exchanges of recipes from the homeland began.
The foundations of traditional Greek cuisine as we know
it in Australia had been formed.

A year into their marriage, and with a new baby girl
(namely me), my parents bought a house in Richmond.
This house was to become home, and still is to this very day.
This *spiti* (meaning 'home') is where I grew up and where
I learnt the importance of family, religion, traditions and,
especially, Greek food. My mother was what is called a
noikokira: a beautiful word derived from *oikos* ('home')
and *kira* ('lady') that frames one's existence in the family
home and community. In my mother's eyes, being a *noikokira*
was the essence of being a woman. It meant that a woman's
primary responsibility was the wellbeing of her family,
and at the cornerstone of that wellbeing was the nourishment
of family and friends through beautiful food made with
only the best ingredients and lots of love.

Our home was where everyone would meet, particularly on weekends.
From a very young age, my mother and father exposed me to the
importance of good-quality ingredients — fresh and seasonal.
On Friday nights, my mum would take me shopping for food:
first to the butchers, and then to the deli where she would
buy her feta cheese, olive oil, cured meats, pulses and so on.
At first, the only deli that existed was Pitsilidis on
Lonsdale Street; it was an institution. Saturday mornings
were spent at the Gleadell Street Market in Richmond,
which still stands today. Once home, she and I (as her
helping hand) would cook, knowing that we would have
many visitors. These get-togethers celebrated name days,
birthdays, religious occasions, weddings and christenings.
Always present was my mum's famous pita (in particular,
Spanakopita). Our guests would also bring plates of food,
each one beautifully decorated, and before you knew it our
big kitchen table would be filled with an abundance of dishes.

During these gatherings, the guests would talk about work,
the homeland and their children, and the women would swap
ideas and recipes. Listening to them always fascinated
and inspired me. I loved hearing all the stories that they
exchanged, some good, some bad, and some sad. The sacrifices
that they made were enormous. I particularly loved listening
to the women meticulously describing their recipes.

I am often astonished by my mother's amazing knowledge of and ability to cook traditional Greek food. At nineteen she was married and at twenty a mother; she had no recipe books to follow. How did she remember it all? Just like her mother had passed this knowledge on to her by involving her in the kitchen and bringing her along on market trips, she passed it on to me from a very young age. In my case, I have always been passionate about Greek cuisine, traditions and culture — not only because of its simplicity, but for the fact that it nourishes the soul. My problem was that, in this fast-paced life that we live, I never had enough time to perfect the skills that my mum wanted to pass on.

In April 2009, everything suddenly changed. I was diagnosed with stage 3 breast cancer. From a timing perspective, it was our Holy Week. Was this symbolic? I didn't know. All I knew was that I was in deep shock. I remember thinking that I had so much more that I wanted to do and so much that I hadn't done yet. My mum would always beg me to practice making pita with her, but there was never enough time. After I came home from the surgery rooms, I wondered how I would tell my family about the cancer diagnosis. As I walked through the front door, I saw my mother dyeing our eggs red — a very important tradition during Holy Week. It was difficult to face her. In a strange way, I felt like I was letting her down. It was my responsibility, as a *noikokira*, to continue our traditions and pass them on to my sons and grandchildren, just as my mother had done with me. But would I survive to fulfil my role?

Difficult days were ahead. Surgery upon surgery, eighteen months of chemotherapy and six weeks of radiation on a daily basis. During this time, I lost my father, a remarkable man who instilled in me the value of education and of knowledge. I also lost my aunt Katina, my mum's sister, whom I adored. She was like a mother to me. She had no children of her own, and from the day she arrived in Australia she nurtured and spoiled me in ways that only an aunty can.

> My most beautiful memories are those created around the kitchen and dinner table.

At the same time, the heroes that migrated to this country in the 1950s and 1960s were slowly ageing and passing away. Seeing the sea of grey hair at church on Sunday mornings or the death notices in *Neos Kosmos* (the Greek Australian newspaper) on Mondays and Thursdays, I felt a sense of urgency. I did not want their sacrifices to be in vain. What defines us as a culture is our food, language and traditions. What sustains us is knowing that the legacy of our parents and grandparents will persist from one generation to another. To understand who we are, we must remember where we came from, how and why. Becoming aware of death and my own mortality forced me to be grateful for what I have — and my most beautiful memories are those created around the kitchen and dinner table. It also made me realise the importance of pursuing your dreams. It was only while being treated for cancer that I made cooking and offering Greek food to all my new mission. I dreamt of opening up a little shop that would serve the best of authentic Greek cuisine.

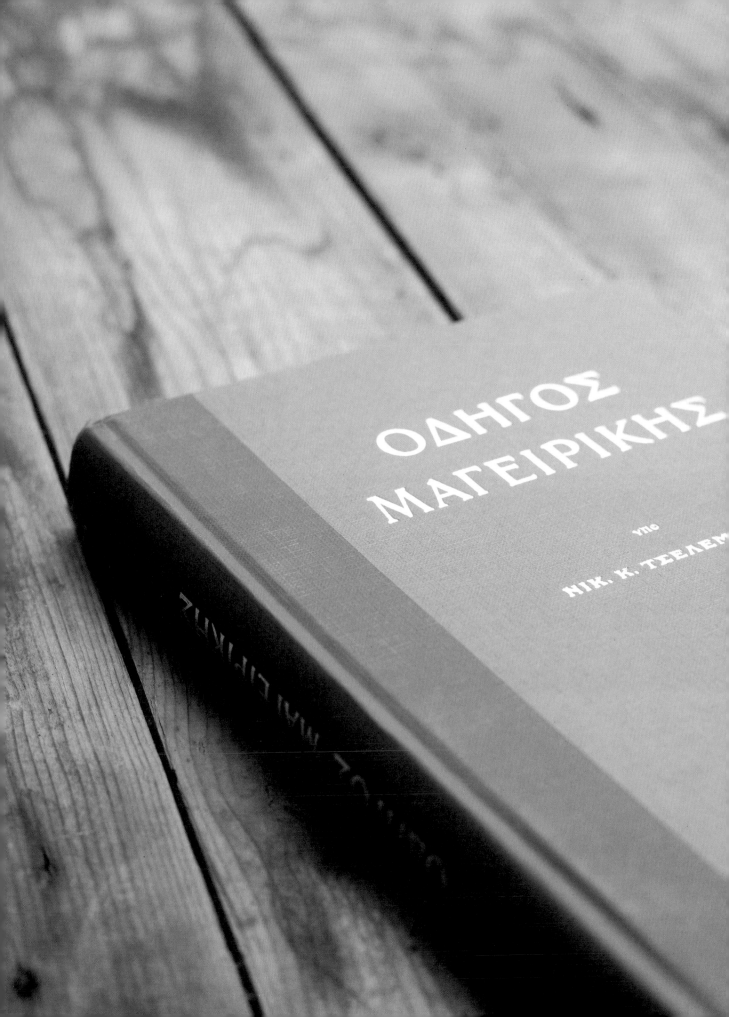

ΟΔΗΓΟΣ
ΜΑΓΕΙΡΙΚΗΣ

υπο

ΝΙΚ. Κ. ΤΣΕΛΕΜ

My dream became a reality when my dear friend Kathy Demos
introduced me to George Christopoulos, who had a similar
vision and dream. Sweet Greek at the Prahran Market was born.
In June 2012, I took ownership of Sweet Greek and the
journey began. This was not to be a store of chargrilled
food, but rather food that we identify with home.
Nothing gives me greater pleasure than customers coming
into the store and commenting that the aroma of the
Spanakopita in the oven reminds them of their mother's
or grandmother's kitchen.

When Mum came to Australia, she wanted a cookbook but
unfortunately couldn't afford it. When many of her relatives
migrated to Australia during the sixties, her one wish was
for them to bring a cookbook. She called this a *Tselemendes*.
So when someone bought her a new edition of a cookbook by
Sofia Skoura, which we used to explore other food and sweets
from everywhere else in Greece, we continued to call
it *Tselemendes*. From our new *Tselemendes*, I remember making
Karithopita (Walnut Cake). It was a great success and I
became popular in our family for it. Everyone would ask
me to make it for celebrations and special events.
It's only now, as an adult, that I realise that *Tselemendes*,
rather than meaning 'cookbook', actually refers to Nikos
Tselemendes, a chef from the 1930s who trained in France and
wrote one of the first influential cookbooks of Greek
cuisine. Nevertheless, Greek cooking as we knew it became
synonymous with *Tselemendes*.

This book — a *Tselemendes* of my own — is a collection
of recipes predominantly from my mother's kitchen:
food that awakens the senses and evokes powerful memories
from my childhood. It also features recipes that I have
collected over the years from friends, neighbours and family.
In this way, I am celebrating them and giving them recognition
as well. The recipes are about celebrating life: taking the
food from our past, cooking it today and passing it on to
younger generations for the future.

Being Greek means that we are always celebrating something,
and this celebration takes place through food, music and wine.

I hope you enjoy my journey.

Kali Orexi

BLESSING OF THE WATERS

TOMATO FRITTERS

MARINATED OLIVES

SOUVLAKIA

TZATZIKI

TIROKAFTERI
FETA DIP

LETTUCE SALAD

STUFFED PEPPERS WITH FETA

The Epiphany is a celebration — firstly of the birth
of Christ, the visit of the Three Wise Men and
Christ's baptism in the Jordan River.

It also commemorates the Blessing of the Waters,
a celebration of new beginnings. A cross is thrown
into the sea and is retrieved by swimmers who are
then entitled to good luck.

We start the day by going to church. We receive holy
water in a bottle, which we all have of sip of,
and then sprinkle it throughout the house so that
it can be blessed for the year ahead.

Psomi (bread), tyri (cheese) and elies (olives) are what
we call the 'Holy Trinity'. They form the foundation
of Greek cuisine. When all else fails, you can sit down
with these three ingredients and, with good company,
have a feast. One of my memories growing up was that,
if ever we were hungry, we would ask Mum what was for
dinner or lunch. She would say, 'Psomi, tyri and elies,'
especially if she hadn't prepared anything.

Olive oil is one of the cornerstones of Greek cuisine.
It is significant in many facets of our culture,
not only for its culinary use but also from a religious
perspective. Olive oil is blessed by the priest and
applied to the child's feet, hands, ears and mouth
in order to dedicate them to the services of God.
Godparents also anoint the baby's entire body in oil.

Along with olives and olive oil, Greek cuisine widely
uses vegetables, particularly eggplant and zucchini;
herbs; grains and bread; wine; fish and various meats,
including poultry, rabbit and pork; as well as cheese
and yoghurt.

The Blessing of the Waters is the simplest of
Greek feasts that gives the greatest pleasure.

PSOMI (BREAD), TYRI (CHEESE)
AND ELIES (OLIVES) ARE WHAT
WE CALL THE 'HOLY TRINITY'.
THEY FORM THE FOUNDATION
OF GREEK CUISINE.

Tomato Fritters

1½ kg ripe tomatoes

4 spring onions,
finely chopped

1 large onion,
finely diced

150 g feta, crumbled

approx. 300g
self-raising flour

1 tsp baking powder

3 tbsp mint,
finely chopped

3 tbsp parsley,
finely chopped

3 tbsp dill,
finely chopped

salt

a pinch of pepper

oil (for frying)

These delicious fritters from the island of Santorini are made with sweet, ripe tomatoes, herbs and feta. They are best served as a mezze snack or light meal with salad. Tzatziki is a great accompaniment.

Take the tomatoes and finely chop them.

Gently squeeze all the seeds out and allow the extra liquid to drain.

Place the tomatoes into a colander and allow them to drain for about an hour.

In a bowl, combine the tomatoes with the onions, mint, parsley, dill, spring onions, salt and pepper. Mix well.

Add the flour and baking powder. The texture will very much depend on the liquid of the tomatoes. Add the crumbled feta into the bowl and mix well. The mixture should resemble a stiff batter. Add more flour if necessary.

Take your frypan and heat about ½ an inch of oil.

Take spoonfuls of batter and fry untill golden. Turn over and fry the other side.

Remove and place on absorbent paper to drain.

Marinated Olives

2 cups of plain olives
(preferably black but
green is okay as well)

4 cloves of garlic,
finely sliced

1 cup of olive oil

2 tbsp red wine vinegar

2 tbsp lemon juice

a pinch of chilli flakes

a good pinch of
dried Greek oregano

sprigs of fresh
lemon thyme

lemon slice (to serve)

Gently warm the olive oil in a pan.

Turn off the heat and add the garlic, vinegar, lemon juice, chilli flakes, oregano and thyme.

Let all these flavours infuse the oil.

Put your olives into a nice bowl. Once the oil has cooled, pour it over the olives.

Let them stand overnight before eating.

Serve with a slice of lemon. You can pour the warm oil over the olives and eat immediately if you wish.

Souvlakia

1 kg pork, lamb
or chicken thigh

2 onions

1 green capsicum

1 red capsicum

2 garlic cloves

grated lemon rind

½ cup of olive oil

approx. 1 cup of red wine

1 tsp sweet paprika

salt and pepper

lemon juice, oregano,
tzatziki, salad and
pita bread (to serve)

Everyone knows what a souvlaki is and no doubt somewhere, somehow, most people would have eaten it at least once. Souvlakia were and are street food in Greece. There are many variations, such as pork, lamb or chicken. They are a real treat and worth going to the effort of cooking them for your family and friends. They are best served with tzatziki, a good traditional Greek salad and pita bread, which can be bought at any good Greek delicatessen.

Cut meat into small cubes. Slice the onions into quarters or eighths depending on how big or small they are. Cut your capsicums into 4 centimetre squares.

In a bowl, marinate your meat with the wine, salt, pepper, paprika, crushed garlic and lemon rind. Marinating overnight is preferable, but even a few hours is okay.

Using wooden skewers that have been soaked in water, arrange meat, capsicums and onions in alternating fashion until they are finished.

Grill or barbecue the skewers.

Squeeze lemon juice generously. Serve hot with tzatziki and salad either in a pita bread or on a nice plate, sprinkled with oregano.

Tzatziki

1 cucumber

3-4 cloves of garlic,
finely grated

1 kg yoghurt (strained)

3 tbsp olive oil
(the best you have)

1 tsp white wine vinegar

1 tbsp lemon juice

½ tsp salt

For this recipe, it is
worthwhile investing
in a muslin cloth
(cheesecloth) with which
to strain the yoghurt
overnight.

Some Greeks add a little
sprinkling of dill with
their tzatziki. If you
like dill, feel free
to do so, too.

Start this recipe the night before.

Line a strainer placed over a bowl with the cheesecloth, add the yoghurt and refrigerate overnight.

Peel, grate and drain the cucumber very well.

In a bowl, add the strained yoghurt, garlic, cucumber, olive oil, vinegar, lemon juice and salt. Mix very well.

Taste. If you are happy with the salt and garlic flavour, put the dip in the fridge for a couple of hours to let the flavours intensify.

Tirokafteri

Feta Dip

500 g good-quality feta

½ cup of ricotta

1 red capsicum

2 long chillies
with the seeds

½ cup of olive oil

1 tbsp red wine vinegar

¼ tsp freshly
ground white pepper

salt (to taste)

chilli flakes
or chilli powder
(to taste)

olives and bread
(to serve)

This particular dip
does not necessarily
have to be smooth.
If you prefer a chunkier
dip, just pulse gently
or even mix everything
together using a fork.

Preheat your griller and grill the capsicum and the chillies
until they blister. Peel them, and drain to remove excess liquid.
Once drained, place them on paper towels.

In your food processor, add the feta with the capsicum, chillies,
pepper and ricotta. Gradually add all the olive oil and vinegar
until it is nice and smooth.

Taste to see whether the dip needs any salt. This will depend
on the flavour of the cheese.

This dip is intended to be spicy, so if the chillies are not
hot enough, add a few chilli flakes or a pinch of chilli powder.

Serve in a bowl with olives and bread.

THE GREEK
- OREGANO from Cre
- Red Wine Vinega
- White Wine Vineg
- The best Olive O
- Tahini
- Tahini Spreads
- Pasta
- Baked Beans
- Roasted Pepper
- Coffee
- Rusks
- Spoon Sweets
- Honey
- Chocolate
- Hand Made HALV

Lettuce Salad

1 large cos lettuce
or 3 baby cos lettuce

3 spring onions,
finely chopped

½ red onion,
finely sliced

5 radishes, thinly sliced

1 continental cucumber,
thinly sliced

4 tbsp feta, crumbled

3 tbsp good-quality
olive oil

1 tbsp white wine vinegar

1 tbsp lemon juice

2 tbsp dill,
finely chopped

salt

Wash lettuce thoroughly. Stack the leaves and roll into a cylinder. With a very sharp knife, finely cut across.

In a big salad bowl, add the chopped lettuce leaves, salt, olive oil, lemon juice, vinegar, radishes, onion, dill and cucumber.

Mix thoroughly, then taste. If necessary, add more vinegar, salt or lemon juice.

Add crumbled feta on top.

Stuffed Peppers
with Feta

15 long pale green or red
peppers

1 hot green chilli,
finely chopped (optional)

3-4 thick slices of
bread, crusts removed,
cut into large cubes

250 g feta, crumbled

1 cup ricotta

2 tbsp olive oil,
plus extra for brushing

1 tbsp fresh parsley,
finely chopped

a pinch of dried oregano

salt

pepper

The chilli is optional.
It can be omitted if
you don't like the heat.

To stuff the peppers you
will need a small spoon,
ideally with a long
handle. A chopstick is
also helpful to push the
filling to the end.

*The long peppers remind me of summer. They are delicious cooked
in so many different ways, but with feta cheese it is one
of my favourite recipes.*

Preheat the grill.

Cut off the tops of the peppers and remove the seeds,
taking care not to pierce the sides. Set aside the tops for
use as decorations for the finished dish.

Create a cheese mixture by combining the feta, olive oil,
oregano and ricotta in a bowl, season with salt and pepper,
and mash with a fork until smooth. Stir in the chilli and parsley.

Fill the peppers with the cheese mixture and insert a cube
of bread to close the opening to prevent the cheese from
leaking during cooking.

Place the peppers on a flameproof dish or roasting pan,
brush with a little olive oil, and cook under the grill, turning so
that all sides are cooked, for 15 minutes. The peppers can also be
cooked in a non-stick frying pan brushed with a little olive oil.

Serve hot or cold. This is a perfect mezze with ouzo.

DAD'S NAME DAY

SPANAKOPITA

CUTLETS

ZUCCHINI FRITTERS

LOULOUTHIA YEMISTA
STUFFED ZUCCHINI FLOWERS

TARAMA

HORIATIKI SALATA
TRADITIONAL GREEK SALAD

SLOW-ROASTED CHICKEN, ARTICHOKES,
PEAS, TOMATOES AND POTATOES

OCTOPUS

THE AFTERNOON OF THE EPIPHANY
IS THE IDEAL TIME FOR ME AND
MUM TO START COOKING AND
PREPARING FOR THE NEXT DAY,
WHICH IS THE NAME DAY OF
YIANNI [JOHN], MY DEAREST DAD.
ON THIS DAY, WE ALSO CELEBRATE
MY SON, JONATHAN, WHO WAS NAMED
AFTER MY FATHER.

NAME DAYS ORIGINATE FROM
THE GREEK ORTHODOX CHURCH'S
CALENDAR OF SAINTS
AND CELEBRATES EACH SAINT'S
NAME WITH A FEAST.

Spanakopita

2 bunches of English
spinach, washed and
finely shredded

½ bunch of spring onion,
finely sliced

dough (see 'Basic Dough'
recipe on page 234)

1 cup of cornflour

300 g feta, or 200 g feta
and 100 g ricotta

3 eggs, slightly beaten

½ cup of olive oil,
plus another 1 cup
for the pastry sheets

2 tbsp dill,
finely sliced

1 tsp salt

½ tsp pepper

sesame seeds
(as garnish)

You will also need
a 40 cm baking tray.

Preheat your oven to 180°C.

Take your dough and divide it into five balls. Allow them to rest for an hour and cover them so they do not dry out.

Oil your baking tray.

Prepare your spinach. Wash it and shred it finely.

Sprinkle 1 teaspoon of salt over the spinach and crush it with your hands. Continue to do this until it has wilted.

Squeeze out the excess liquid and place the spinach in a big bowl. Grind some pepper into the spinach.

Crumble the feta and ricotta into the spinach. Add the dill and mix well. Taste to see if more salt is needed.

Add slightly beaten eggs and mix again. Put aside.

Using a rolling pin, roll each pastry ball into a circular sheet, constantly adding cornflour on top to stop it from sticking. Make it nice and fine, almost translucent.

Drizzle each sheet with olive oil and fold over to form a semi-circle. Spoone one fifth of the spinach mixture along the straight edge of your pastry, leaving a ½ inch border. Roll it up carefully, stretch it a little, and form a coil starting from the centre of the baking tray.

Brush the top with olive oil and sprinkle with sesame seeds. Bake for 45 minutes.

Cutlets

2 kg lamb cutlets,
trimmed of all fat —
ask your butcher
to do this

½ cup of olive oil

juice of 2 lemons

1 tsp oregano

1 tsp salt

pepper, freshly ground

Greek salad and tzatziki
(to serve)

You can also mix all
the ingredients together
and marinate the cutlets
before grilling. I prefer
to drizzle the olive oil
on after grilling,
together with the oregano
and lemon juice. The best
results and flavour of
course come from using
a barbecue with briquette
or Mallee Root charcoal.
This ensures a lovely
chargrilled result for
your meat. Nonetheless,
when pressed for time,
a gas barbecue will also
work well for cutlets,
as will any griller.

One of the highlights of summer is the availability of sweet succulent lamb. As I stated in my Cook's Note, I always use Salt Bush lamb, but any organic variety will be fine.

Place cutlets in a baking dish. Sprinkle the salt and pepper all over, massaging them into the meat.

Drizzle 2 tablespoons from the olive oil allocation onto your meats.

Barbecue the cutlets, turning carefully to ensure they do not burn.

When all cutlets are cooked, sprinkle with oregano and drizzle the lemon juice and the rest of the olive oil.

Serve with Greek salad and tzatziki.

Zucchini Fritters

2-4 medium zucchinis

4 spring onions,
finely sliced

1 brown onion,
finely diced or grated

approx. 2½ cups
of self-raising flour

1 tsp baking powder

½ cup of feta, crumbled

3 eggs

oil (for frying)

1 cup of milk

3 tbsp parsley,
finely chopped

3 tbsp mint,
finely chopped

1 tbsp dill,
finely chopped

1 tsp salt

¼ tsp pepper,
freshly ground

Serve warm with
tzatziki and salad.
The fritters can
also be eaten cold.

*During spring and summer we make the most of zucchinis,
as they are in season and can be used and prepared in
so many different ways. Zucchini Fritters are a family favourite.
They are a great light snack and are delicious in kids' lunchboxes.
Growing up, Mum would often make these fritters and pack
them for our lunch.*

Grate the zucchinis into a colander. Sprinkle some salt on top,
leave for 30 mintes to allow any excess liquid to drain out.

Using your hands, squeeze them thoroughly to remove remaining
moisture.

Grate the onion, chop the herbs and spring onions, and place
these in a bowl. Then, add in all the other ingredients and mix
thoroughly. The mixture should look like a thick pancake batter.
If it's too runny, add some more flour.

Heat half an inch of oil in a shallow, wide pan and place spoonfuls
of the mixture into the oil.

Fry until golden on one side, and then turn to cook the other side.

Loulouthia Yemista
Stuffed Zucchini Flowers

30 zucchini flowers

Filling

2 tomatoes, finely grated

1 onion, grated

4 cloves of garlic, finely grated

1 cup of short-grain rice

1 cup of olive oil

1 cup of parsley, finely chopped

a few sprigs of mint leaves, finely chopped

To cook

juice of 1 lemon

2 cups of water

1 tsp salt

½ tsp ground pepper

Zucchini flowers stuffed with rice are a true delicacy and not that difficult to make. We anxiously await every summer for the zucchini plants to produce their flowers. We pick them early in the morning, wash them and stack them like little hats ready to be filled. My boys can sit down and devour an entire baking dish filled with little flowers.

Wash and drain the zucchini flowers. The flowers are delicate so be careful!

Preheat the oven to 180°C.

Put all filling ingredients into a bowl and mix them well. Very carefully fill the flowers with the mixture using a spoon and then close the tops with their own endings. I find twisting the tops the best way to secure them.

Place the flowers carefully and snugly in a baking dish. Add 2 cups of water, the juice of a lemon and a drizzle of olive oil. Bake for 30 minutes.

Tarama

150 g white fish roe

4 thick slices
of stale bread,
crust removed

½ small brown onion

1 L grapeseed oil
(or sunflower oil)

juice of 2 lemons

Yes, Tarama is that pink stuff that you can find at all the delis and supermarkets. My Tarama, however, is made with white fish roe. The end result is a white, glossy dip. At the Sweet Greek stall, I make Tarama weekly; sometimes I can't keep up with the demand. It is worth sourcing the white roe.

I first learnt to make Tarama by watching my dear Aunt Koula. In the seventies, my auntie, who is married to my uncle Paul (Dad's brother), entertained whenever she could. She was a social butterfly and mingled a lot. As such, she was always learning new recipes. Tarama was one of them, and I have always made it as she taught me back then.

Soak the bread in water until it becomes soft. Drain and squeeze with your hands.

Using a food processor, blend the fish roe, bread and onion until you get a nice smooth paste.

With the food processor still running, gradually add the oil and lemon juice, alternating the two. Don't rush this stage. Ensure that the oil is poured in a gentle stream.

Your dip is ready to serve when it forms a luscious, smooth paste that will be almost like a mousse.

Horiatiki Salata
Traditional Greek Salad

4 sweet ripe tomatoes

1 continental cucumber, peeled (unless you obtained it from your garden, in which case leave the skin on)

1 Spanish red onion

2-3 tbsp kalamata olives

200 g good-quality Greek feta

½ cup extra virgin olive oil (the best that you have)

1 tsp red wine vinegar

½ cup lemon juice

½ tsp Greek dried oregano

½ tsp salt

crusty bread (to serve)

Horiatiki Salata is a classic salad familiar to all. It is very simple, but its success relies heavily on the use of the freshest seasonal ingredients: ripe, sweet aromatic tomatoes; crisp cucumber; luscious green capsicums, firm kalamata olives; and salty, smooth feta cheese. This salad can be served with any meal at any time, or even as a meal in itself.

Slice the tomatoes, cucumbers and capsicum. Try to make them all an even size.

Slice the red onion into thin rings and soak it in the lemon juice for about half an hour.

Assemble all the ingredients together in a bowl.

Sprinkle the oregano and finish off with the red wine vinegar, salt and olive oil.

Mix well, then crumble feta cheese on top.

Slow-roasted Chicken, Artichokes, Peas, Tomatoes and Potatoes

4 chicken Marylands
or 6 chicken thighs

4 globe artichokes

½ kg frozen peas
or 1 kg fresh peas

1 kg ripe tomatoes,
peeled, seeded and
finely chopped;
or 400 g canned
chopped tomatoes

1 kg potatoes,
peeled and quartered

2 red onions,
quartered then sliced

1 lemon, halved

1 tbsp plain flour

1 cup of olive oil

1 tbsp freshly squeezed
lemon juice

1 handful of fresh
parsley, chopped

1 tsp sugar

1 tsp salt

¼ tsp pepper

An easier method to cook
the above meal is to put
all the ingredients into
a baking dish and mix
thoroughly. Cover the
dish and then bake in the
oven for about an hour at
180°C.

Frozen artichokes are
now available and can be
substituted for the fresh
ones, especially when the
latter are not available.

Cut off the artichoke stems about 2 inches from the base, trim the bases, remove all the thick green leaves and the chokes, leaving only the cup-shaped hearts. Cut these in half and rub with the lemon halves to prevent discolouration. Place them in a bowl of water mixed with the flour and lemon juice. Leave aside until ready to be used.

Pour a little olive oil into a non-stick pan and brown your chicken pieces. Remove them from the pan.

Add the onion and cook over low heat for 5 minutes, stirring occasionally until softened.

Add the tomatoes, sugar, parsley, salt and pepper.

Return the chicken pieces and gently simmer for 30 minutes.

Add the artichoke hearts, potatoes and peas. Cover and simmer for 1 hour until the vegetables are tender and the sauce has reduced.

Octopus

1 octopus
(approx. 2 kg —
it doesn't matter
if it's bigger)

2 cloves of garlic,
finely sliced

1 big red chilli,
finely sliced

1 cup of olive oil

½ cup of vinegar

½ cup of lemon juice

oregano, finely chopped

2 bay leaves

10 peppercorns

I like to fill a big
jar and use it when
we feel like some
octopus or as part
of a mezze platter.
Ensure that it is
covered well with
the oil.

Once your octopus has been cleaned by your fishmonger,
take it home and wash it again thoroughly.

Put your octopus in a large pot, cover it and cook gently for
approximately 30-40 minutes. Do not add anything at this stage.
The octopus will release a lot of liquid.

Add the peppercorns, vinegar and bay leaves. If the pot
has dried, add a cup of water. Cook until the octopus is tender
(perhaps another 30 minutes). You will need to check it.

Remove from the heat and let it cool. Once cool, slice the octopus
into small pieces, diagonally across.

In a large bowl, add the octopus, lemon juice, garlic, chilli and oregano.
Mix well and then add the olive oil.

The olive oil should cover the octopus completely, so add more
if necessary.

Taste to see whether it needs more salt or lemon juice.
It should be slightly tangy.

IT'S STILL SUMMER,
THE FORMAL FESTIVITIES
ARE OVER, AND NOW IT'S TIME
TO CELEBRATE AND RELAX
WITH THE FAMILY.

SUMMER FAMILY FEAST

YEMISTA
STUFFED VEGETABLES WITH MEAT

PSARI PLAKI STO FOURNO
BAKED SNAPPER WITH HERBS AND POTATOES

BAMIES
SLOW-COOKED OKRA CASSEROLE

TIGANITA KOLOKITHIA
FRIED ZUCCHINI

ANGINARES ME ARAKA KE KOUKIA
ARTICHOKES WITH PEAS AND BROAD BEANS

Yemista

Stuffed Vegetables with Meat

500 g minced meat
(preferably beef)

3 large tomatoes

2 red capsicums

1 green capsicum

2 small round zucchinis

1 large eggplant

2 large potatoes,
cut into wedges

1 cup of feta, crumbled

2 large onions, grated

5 cloves of garlic,
crushed

2 cups of
short-grain rice

1 cup of olive oil

1 cup of water

2 tbsp tomato paste

½ cup of mint,
freshly chopped

½ cup of parsley,
freshly chopped

½ cup of basil,
freshly chopped

1 tsp oregano

¼ tsp cinnamon

¼ tsp allspice

1-2 tsp salt

½ tsp pepper

To make the vegetarian
version of Yemista,
follow the same process.
However, you will have
to add a further ½ cup
of rice.

*Seasonal vegetables like tomatoes, capsicums, eggplant and
zucchini are stuffed with rice and herbs then served as a main meal.
The vegetables can either be prepared with rice and fresh herbs,
or with minced meat, rice and herbs. Either way, they are delicious
and reflect summer on a plate.*

Preheat the oven to 180°C.

Slice off and put aside the tops of the tomatoes, capsicums,
and zucchini. Scoop out the pulp from the tomatoes and zucchini
with a spoon, and keep these for later. Seed the capsicums
without piercing the skin. Sprinkle the interior of the vegetables'
'shells' with a little salt and set aside.

Cut the eggplant in half lengthwise and scoop out most of the
flesh to form two shells.

Blanch the eggplant and the capsicums in boiling water for
about 3 minutes and drain.

Arrange all the vegetables in a baking dish. Finely chop all the
flesh that has been scooped out from the tomatoes, zucchini
and eggplant. Heat half the olive oil in a pan over high heat. Add
your meat and cook until brown. Add the onion and the garlic and
all the flesh from your vegetables. Cook this mixture for about
5 minutes, stirring frequently. Add your rice, cinnamon, allspice
and oregano together with the tomato paste. Take off the heat
and add all your fresh herbs and feta.

Spoon the mixture into the vegetable shells until they are
three-quarters full and replace the tops on the tomatoes,
capsicums and zucchini.

On a baking dish, arrange the stuffed vegetables and put potato
wedges in between them. Sprinkle a little salt, pour in about 1 cup
of water and then drizzle the remaining olive oil all over. Bake in a
moderate oven for about 1½-2 hours. Check halfway. If the tops
brown too quickly, cover loosely with aluminium foil.

Serve hot or at room temperature.

Psari Plaki Sto Fourno
Baked Snapper with Herbs and Potatoes

1 medium snapper

4 potatoes, peeled and
cut into wedges or slices
(approx. ½ inch thick)

1 can of tomatoes

6 spring onions,
thinly sliced

2 onions, thinly sliced

5-6 cloves of garlic,
crushed

1 cup of olive oil

½ bunch of parsley or
dill, finely chopped

a pinch of sweet paprika

2 bay leaves

1 tsp salt

pepper, freshly ground

You can also
prepare this dish
with filleted fish.

Cooking whole fish on the bone is the tastiest way of preparing fish. With this dish, the potatoes take on the flavours of the fish, herbs and tomatoes. It is absolutely delicious.

Preheat the oven to 180°C.

Using a sharp knife, score the fish across the body in three places. Do this on both sides. The scoring ensures that the fish absorbs all the flavours and cooks evenly.

In a large frypan, sauté the onions with a little olive oil. Add the garlic, then the spring onions, bay leaves, sweet paprika and tomatoes.

Cook this for approximately 10-15 minutes to allow the flavours to combine while also reducing the liquid.

Season it with a little salt and pepper.

Place the fish in a baking tray and assemble the potatoes around the fish.

Carefully spoon the sauce all over the fish and inside the scored cavities. Drizzle some of the sauce onto and around the potatoes and mix well.

Pour the remaining olive oil over the fish and potatoes. Sprinkle half of the parsley or dill on top.

Bake in a moderate oven for about 30-45 minutes. To ensure that the snapper does not burn, moisten some baking paper and place on top. Add half a glass of water and continue baking if the sauce appears to be drying out at any stage.

Once the potatoes and fish have cooked, sprinkle them with the rest of the parsley or dill and serve.

Bamies

Slow-cooked Okra Casserole

¾ kg fresh okra

1 onion, cut into slices

1 tin of tomatoes

1 cup of extra virgin
olive oil

1 tsp red wine vinegar

a few sprigs of parsley,
finely chopped

a pinch of chilli flakes

a pinch of sweet paprika

½ tsp sugar

1 tsp salt

pepper, freshly ground

It's summer and, along with all the other scrumptious vegetables, okra is in season. Okra is a real favourite in Greece and can be cooked as a vegetable casserole or with chicken. Either way, it's delicious. When they are not in season, the tinned variety or even the frozen kind is just as good.

When preparing okra, keep them whole and carefully cut off the conical head from each pod. Be careful not to cut too deep and expose the seeds. Remove the black tip at the other end and rinse thoroughly. (If you are using tinned okra, these steps can be omitted.)

Sauté the onions in a shallow pan with olive oil. Stir in the tomatoes, chilli, paprika, sugar, salt and pepper. Cook for 5 minutes.

Add the vinegar, then the okra, and shake the pan. Do not stir as this may break up the okra and expose the seeds.

The okra should be completely submerged in the sauce so you may have to add a little water.

Cook gently for 30-40 minutes and finish off by adding the parsley.

Tiganita Kolokithia

Fried Zucchinis

1 kg zucchinis

plain flour

vegetable oil
(for deep-frying)

a pinch of salt

mizithra*

*Mizithra is a delicious
salty hard cheese used
in pasta dishes as well
as grated on vegetables.

Slice the zucchinis into circles.

Using a freezer bag, pour in some flour and add a pinch of salt.

Add the zucchini slices to the freezer bag containing flour.
Shake gently to coat the slices.

In a deep pot, heat your vegetable oil and deep-fry the
zucchini slices until golden. After removing them from the oil,
place them on paper towels.

Arrange them on a platter and grate mizithra on top.

Anginares Me
Araka Ke Koukia

Artichokes with Peas
and Broad Beans

4 globe artichokes

½ kg broad beans,
freshly shelled

1 kg peas,
freshly shelled

6 spring onions,
thinly sliced

1 onion, thinly sliced

1 cup of extra virgin
olive oil

juice of 1½ lemons

2 cups of water

1 tsp cooking salt

1 tsp pepper
(preferably white)

1 tbsp fennel leaves,
finely chopped
(to serve)

When fresh ingredients
are not available,
the frozen variety
will be fine.

*The combination of artichokes, peas and broad beans,
together with the fennel, is absolutely delicious.*

Cut off the artichoke stems about 2 inches from the base, trim the
bases, remove all the thick green leaves and the chokes, leaving
only the cup-shaped hearts.

Using a wide shallow pan, sauté the onion and the spring onions.
Add the peas, broad beans and artichokes. Stir to allow the oil
and onions to mix through.

Add the lemon juice, water, salt and pepper. Cover your pan.

Cook for about 45 minutes on low heat, stirring occasionally.
Check to ensure that there is enough water. You want the liquid
to thicken into a light sauce.

Once the vegetables are cooked, sprinkle the fennel on top.

INDEPENDENCE DAY
25 MARCH

TIGANITES ZARGANES
FRIED GARFISH

POTATOES WITH LEMON AND OREGANO

FAVA
CHICKPEA OR YELLOW SPLIT PEA DIP

MELITSANOSALATA
EGGPLANT DIP

HORTA
LEAFY GREENS

THE GREEK NATIONAL ANNIVERSARY
OF INDEPENDENCE DAY,
ALSO CALLED 'EVANGELISMOS',
COMMEMORATES GREECE'S VICTORY
IN THE WAR OF INDEPENDENCE
AGAINST TURKEY. ON THIS DAY,
WE TRADITIONALLY EAT FISH,
AND MY DAD ESPECIALLY LOVED
GARFISH AND SKORTHALIA
[GARLIC DIP] ACCOMPANIED BY
HORTA [BOILED GREEN VEGETABLES]
AND SALAD.

THE FIRST GREEK ORTHODOX
CHURCH BUILT IN MELBOURNE,
SITUATED ON VICTORIA PARADE,
EAST MELBOURNE,
IS NAMED EVANGELISMO.
IT WAS HERE THAT MY
MUM AND DAD WERE MARRIED.
IT WAS ALSO THE CHURCH
WHERE I WAS CHRISTENED,
AND, IN FOLLOWING TRADITION,
WHERE I WAS MARRIED
AND WHERE LATER MY BOYS
WERE CHRISTENED.

Tiganites Zarganes

Fried Garfish

1-2 kg garfish
(ask your fishmonger to
clean them — some people
remove the heads but
I like them left on)

2 cups of plain flour

sunflower oil
(for frying)

juice of 2-3 lemons
(depending on how
juicy they are)

1 tsp dried oregano

1 tsp cooking salt

pepper, freshly cracked
(to taste)

Garfish is a deliciously sweet fish that is easy to clean. When introducing fish to my sons, it was garfish that I cooked — firstly because of its flavour, and secondly because you only have to remove one backbone.

What my dad would do for some garfish and a plate of Horta!

The easiest way to begin this recipe is to fill a freezer bag with the flour, salt, pepper and oregano.

Heat the oil in a large frypan.

Place a few garfish at a time into the bag with the flour. Dust off any excess, then fry them in the hot oil until the skin is nice and golden, turning over once only. If you find that the oil's heat is too much, reduce the flame a little.

Arrange them on a platter like little soldiers and serve with a plate of Horta (leafy green vegetables), potato salad and crusty bread. A squeeze of lemon juice is also essential.

Potatoes with Lemon and Oregano

1-2 kg potatoes,
peeled and rinsed

6 tbsp olive oil

juice of 1 large lemon
(you can add more
depending on what you
will be serving the
potatoes with)

water

1 heaped tsp
dried oregano

You will also need
a non-stick ovenproof
dish of about 22 × 30 cm.

Preheat the oven to 180°C.

Halve the potatoes lengthwise then cut each half into two
or three gondolas, depending on the size of your potatoes.
Spread them onto the ovenproof dish.

Splash the lemon juice and olive oil over the potatoes,
and sprinkle salt and pepper generously. Crush the oregano
between your fingers, letting it fall over the potatoes.

Turn the potatoes to coat them well with everything.
Dribble the water down the sides of the dish to about ½ an inch
high and give it a shuffle.

Roast for about 1 ½ hours until the potatoes are tender,
melting and a bit golden here and there, with still a bit
of sauce in the dish. You will need to turn and baste
them every 20 minutes or so.

Serve hot and add more salt and pepper to taste.

Fava

Chickpea or Yellow Split Pea Dip

½ kg chickpeas
or yellow split peas

1 stick of celery,
finely sliced

1 large onion,
finely diced

3 shallots,
finely sliced

1 cup of olive oil

1 cup of lemon juice

water (for boiling)

1 tsp dried oregano

3 bay leaves

salt

pepper

If using chickpeas soak
overnight.

Fava should have a delicious earthy flavour. It is best enjoyed with crusty bread and olives.

Wash the chickpeas or yellow split peas thoroughly.
Put them in a large pot with water, making sure that
they are completely submerged.

Add the bay leaves, onion and celery, then bring them to a boil.

Clean off any scum that appears on the surface of the water.

Continue boiling for about an hour, stirring from time to time.
It is ready when the peas are soft and break down into a puree —
a bit like mashed potatoes.

If the mixture dries up during the cooking process,
add a little more water.

Remove from the heat and take out the bay leaves. Add the oil,
lemon juice, salt and pepper. It should be a little tangy.

Add the dried oregano and serve in a bowl with a drizzle
of olive oil.

At the same time, finely slice the shallots and deep-fry them.
When crispy, sprinkle on top of the Fava. You may add raw
shallots on top as well.

Melitsanosalata
Eggplant Dip

1 kg eggplants

1 red capsicum

½ cup of walnuts,
toasted and finely ground

1 tbsp tahini

2-3 cloves of garlic,
crushed

½ cup of olive oil

2 tbsp red wine vinegar

2 tbsp lemon juice

2-3 tbsp parsley, chopped

a pinch of chilli flakes

1 tsp cooking salt

pepper

If you like a smooth
paste, mix all
ingredients using
a food processor.

Preheat the oven to 200°C.

Place your eggplants in a big baking dish, and in a separate dish place your capsicum.

Cook both vegetables until their skins are kind of charred or brown and the flesh is soft.

Remove them from the oven and, while still hot, peel the outer skin off both the capsicum and the eggplants.

Once peeled, put them into a strainer to allow all the excess liquid to drain.

Once drained, chop them up roughly. Add the walnuts, tahini, salt and pepper.

Stir the mixture with a wooden spoon and gradually add the oil in a steady stream. Then add the vinegar, lemon juice, garlic, chilli flakes and parsley.

Taste. If necessary, add more salt, vinegar or lemon juice.

Horta

Leafy Greens

2 bunches of chicory

1 cup of extra
virgin olive oil
(the best that you have)

juice of 1-2 lemons
(depending on how
tangy you'd like
the Horta to be)

½ tsp salt

Horta can be eaten as
a side dish or as a main
meal with feta cheese and
crusty bread. We like
to serve them with fish.

Vegetables play an important part in Greek cuisine, and among the wide range of traditional vegetarian dishes are what we call Horta (which, translated literally, means 'grass').

Horta can be of the wild variety and the domestically grown. Two varieties that you may be familiar with, which can be bought at your local greengrocer, are chicory and radicchia, as well as curly endive.

For this recipe we will be using chicory, as it is the one that is most widely available at greengrocers.

Cut the chicory into strips approximately 4-5 inches long and wash them thoroughly.

Using a large saucepan, bring some water to a boil and then add the chicory pieces.

Simmer them gently until the stalks are tender. They don't take too long.

Drain and, while still hot, dress them with the salt, olive oil and lemon juice.

Enjoy them however you want.

BEFORE THE FORTY-DAY
FAST OF LENT,
WE INDULGE IN OUR
FAVOURITE DISHES.

FAMILY FEAST BEFORE LENT

CHICKPEA SOUP

SARTHELES
MARINATED SARDINES

KOTA KOKKINISTI ME HILOPITES
CHICKEN CASSEROLE WITH HILOPITES PASTA

BRIAMI
SUMMER VEGETABLE ROAST

PATSARA

Chickpea Soup

500 g dried chickpeas, soaked in cold water overnight

1-2 sticks of celery, finely chopped

1 large onion, chopped

150 mL extra virgin olive oil, plus extra for serving

juice of 1 lemon, or more if needed

2 tbsp fresh flat-leaf parsley, chopped

a sprinkling of dried oregano

1 bay leaf

salt

ground black pepper

I often cook this soup in a pressure cooker, which is particularly useful if I have forgotten to soak the chickpeas. If you have one, use it.

Chickpea Soup has an earthy flavour and nourishes the soul. It is definitely a favourite with family. Crusty bread is a must with this soup, as are feta cheese and olives if desired.

Heat the olive oil in a heavy pan, add the onion and sauté until it starts to colour.

Meanwhile, drain the chickpeas, rinse them under cold water and drain them again. Shake the colander or sieve to dry the chickpeas as much as possible, then add them to the pan. Turn them with a spatula for a few minutes to coat them well with the oil.

Add the celery and bay leaf, then pour in enough hot water to submerge the contents of the pot by about 4 centimetres.

Bring to a boil. Skim off any white froth that rises to the surface using a slotted spoon. Lower the heat, add some pepper, cover and cook for 1-1¼ hours or until the chickpeas are soft.

When the chickpeas are perfectly soft, add the lemon juice. Mix well, then add salt and pepper to taste. Cover the pan and cook gently for 5-10 minutes more, stirring occasionally.

To thicken the soup slightly, take out about two cupfuls of the chickpeas and blend them in a food processor. Make sure the chickpeas are broken up but remain slightly rough. Stir this into the soup and mix well.

Add the parsley and oregano, then taste the soup. If it seems a little bland, add more lemon juice, salt and pepper.

Serve in heated bowls and offer extra olive oil at the table for drizzling on top of the soup.

Sartheles
Marinated Sardines

1 kg fresh sardines

garlic, finely sliced

sunflower oil
(or grapeseed oil)

2 cups of white vinegar

parsley, finely chopped

1½ cups of cooking salt

This can be kept
in the refrigerator
and used as part
of a mezze platter.

Clean the fish and remove the spines and heads. Wash them well and pat dry.

In a large bowl, start to layer the fish, with a layer of salt between each layer, until all the fish is used.

Pour in the vinegar and cover. Ensure the sardines are fully submerged.

Refrigerate for 2-3 days to ensure that the fish have marinated and taken on the flavours of the salt and vinegar.

Remove the sardines from the marinade mixture and place them in a clean container. Add the parsley and garlic.

Cover with sunflower oil or grapeseed oil.

Kota Kokkinisti
Me Hilopites
Chicken Casserole with Hilopites Pasta

6 chicken thighs

500 g hilopites

500 g fresh tomatoes,
peeled and pureed,
or 400 g canned
tomatoes, pureed

2 small onions, grated

4 cloves of garlic,
crushed

5 tbsp olive oil

1 tbsp red wine vinegar

1 bay leaf

1 tiny pinch of cinnamon

1 tsp sugar

salt

pepper

I always rinse my cooked
pasta, no matter what
shape or size, as I
find that this prevents
the pasta from becoming
gluggy.

This is comfort food at its best. Hilopites are a square egg pasta similar to rissoni. All over Greece, small home and artisan businesses produce fabulous homemade hilopites.

For me and my family, summer is the time to prepare the hilopites for the year. We all get together, make the dough using the freshest organic eggs, roll it out and cut it into squares. We then dry the pasta out and store them for the year ahead. We also add this pasta to soups.

In Australia, hilopites are available at all good Greek provedore shops.

Heat the oil in a large pan.

Add the chicken and cook over medium heat, turning frequently, for 8–10 minutes until lightly browned all over. Remove with a slotted spoon and set aside.

Add the onion and garlic to the pan and cook over low heat, stirring occasionally, for 5 minutes until softened. Do not burn.

Return the chicken to the pan. Pour in the tomatoes, add the cinnamon, bay leaf, vinegar and sugar, and season with salt and pepper. Cover and simmer for about 1 hour, or until the chicken is cooked through and the sauce is thick and glossy.

Cook the hilopites in a pot of boiling water by allowing to boil for 5 minutes. Drain and rinse with cold water.

Pour the hilopites into the chicken mixture and stir.

Allow to rest for about 10–15 minutes so that all the flavours can come together. Drizzle with a little more olive oil if you choose.

Briami

Summer Vegetable Roast

2 eggplants

4 zucchinis

4-5 large potatoes, peeled

4 large, firm and ripe tomatoes

1 large red capsicum

1 stalk of celery

2 Spanish red onions

1 chilli, seeded and finely chopped

4-5 cloves of garlic

1 cup of olive oil

2 cups of chicken stock

lemon juice

1 tbsp sweet paprika

1 bay leaf

1 tsp salt

¼ tsp pepper, freshly ground

a good handful' each of fresh mint, basil and parsley, finely chopped (if you don't like basil and mint, just use parsley)

Briami is a traditional dish prepared all over Greece. The tradition continues here in Australia. A summer dish that is easy and delicious, it is served as a main course.

Preheat your oven to 180°C.

Wash your vegetables thoroughly. Cut them all into uniform pieces of about the same size.

Combine the vegetables, onion, garlic, olive oil, salt, pepper, paprika, chilli, bay leaf and stock into a large baking dish and mix well with your hands.

Cover with foil and bake for 30 minutes. Take the foil off and cook for a further 30 minutes. When the vegetables have cooked and caramelised, remove from the oven.

While still hot, drizzle with a little lemon juice and sprinkle all the fresh herbs.

Patsara

Base

400 g polenta

125 g self-raising flour

1 tsp baking powder

¼ cup of sunflower oil

2 cups of boiling water

1 tsp salt

butter (for greasing
the pie dish)

Filling

1 thick bunch or
2 small bunches
of English spinach

1 onion

150 g feta

150 g ricotta

2 tbsp flour

3 eggs

¼ cup of sunflower oil

1 cup of milk

1 tsp salt

½ tsp pepper

My sons called this dish 'Spinach Quiche' when they were little. It's a traditional dish that uses polenta as a base. My mother had forgotten about this dish until her sister visited many years ago and reminded her.

Prepare your spinach by washing it and finely shredding it.

Sprinkle salt over it and crush it with your hands,
continuing to do so until the spinach has wilted.

Squeeze out any excess liquid and place the spinach in a big bowl.

Dice the onion and sauté it in the oil until it is translucent.

Spoon the onion into the spinach while it is hot. This will wilt
the spinach further.

Grind some pepper into the spinach and allow to cool.

While the spinach is cooling, make your base. In a big bowl,
pour in the polenta, boiled water and salt. Stir vigorously,
making sure there are no lumps.

Add the flour, oil and baking powder, and mix until a soft dough
is formed. Add more flour if necessary.

Grease a 40-centimetre pie dish with butter. Pour in the polenta mixture
and, using your hands, press it into the dish. Ensure that a lip is formed up
the sides of the dish, giving it the appearance of a pastry case.

Crumble the feta and ricotta into the spinach. Mix well.
Taste to see if more salt is needed and add salt accordingly.

Add the oil and eggs slightly beaten and mix again.

Pour the spinach and cheese mixture into the base and flatten
with your hands.

Sprinkle 2 tablespoons of flour on top and then half a cup of milk
to moisten the flour. This will form a crust.

Bake at 180°C for approximately 45 minutes.

Use the other half cup of the milk to continue to moisten the
crust as it bakes.

You will know it is ready because the polenta will be golden and crusty.

LENT

FASOULAKIA
GREEN BEAN CASSEROLE

FASOULATHA

SPANAKORIZO
SPINACH WITH RICE

FAKES
LENTIL SOUP

LAHANORIZO
CABBAGE WITH RICE

IMAM BALDI
STUFFED EGGPLANTS

GIGANTES

MAVROMATIKA FASOLIA ME SPANAKIA
BLACK-EYED BEANS WITH SPINACH

THE FESTIVITIES OF CHRISTMAS
AND NEW YEAR ARE BARELY
OVER WHEN WE START ALL OVER
AGAIN FOR LENT AND EASTER.
THE CELEBRATIONS START ON
'KATHARI THEFTERA [CLEAN MONDAY],
WHICH MARKS THE END
OF THE FESTIVITIES KNOWN
AS THE APOKRIES AND THE
COMMENCEMENT OF SARACOSTI [LENT].
ON THIS DAY, GREEKS WISH EACH
OTHER 'KALI SARAKOSTI'
MEANING 'MAY THE PERIOD
OF LENT BE GOOD', AND IN GREECE
IT IS CUSTOMARY TO FLY KITES.

DURING THE 40-DAY PERIOD OF LENT,
WE COOK MEALS THAT CONTAIN
NO MEAT OR ANY ANIMAL-BASED PRODUCTS.
NONETHELESS, THERE ARE STILL
SO MANY DISHES TO CHOOSE FROM!
IT IS A PERIOD OF CLEANSING
AND A TIME TO REFLECT.
WE PREPARE OURSELVES
FOR THE HOLY COMMUNION.

Fasoulakia
Green Bean Casserole

1½ kg green beans

3 zucchinis

3 potatoes

1 carrot

1 can of crushed tomatoes

1 tbsp tomato paste

1 small chilli, seeded and finely chopped (optional)

2 onions, chopped

1 cup of olive oil

3 cups of vegetable stock or water

1 cup of parsley, finely chopped

1 tbsp sweet paprika

salt

pepper

Slice the tops off the green beans and string them if necessary. Rinse and drain, keeping them in your colander for now.

Slice the zucchinis, carrots and chilli. Peel your potatoes and cut them into quarters.

Heat the olive oil in a large non-stick pot and sauté the onions until they are softened and almost sticky (but not burnt).

Add the tomatoes, tomato paste, parsley, two to three grinds of fresh pepper and a good amount of salt and paprika. Simmer uncovered over medium heat for around 10 minutes until the tomatoes soften and collapse.

Add the chilli, potatoes and carrots, then add the stock and put the lid on the saucepan.

When it comes to a boil, stir through the beans and then put the lid back on. Simmer for 30 minutes or until the beans are soft and the liquid has reduced. Add the zucchini and continue to simmer. It's a good idea to stir the beans every so often. At the end of this time there should be a good amount of thickish sauce.

Turn off the heat and leave the casserole covered for a while, allowing it to absorb the flavours.

Serve hot, warm or cold.

Fasoulatha

500 g small
dried white beans,
soaked in cold water
overnight and drained

1 small stalk of celery,
sliced and with leaves
set aside

2 carrots, sliced

1 can of tomatoes

1 small dried red chilli,
crushed (optional)

1 red chilli,
seeded and chopped
(optional)

1 large onion,
finely chopped

½ cup (120 mL)
of olive oil

1 tbsp tomato paste

4 cups (1 L) of hot water

pepper

olives, pickled
vegetables, and cheese
(to serve)

Fasoulatha is the national dish of Greece. Made with white (haricot or cannellini) beans and usually with a hint of chilli, it can be served all year round but is most popular in winter. It can be served with olives, cheese and bread. Pickled vegetables are another good accompaniment.

Rinse the beans, put them in a large pan, and pour in cold water so they are submerged. Bring to a boil, cover, and simmer for around 30 minutes until almost tender. Drain, rinse and set aside.

Meanwhile, heat the oil in a large heavy pan. Add the onion and cook over low heat, stirring occasionally, for about 5 minutes until soft and translucent. Crush the tomatoes and add, along with the tomato paste. Add the carrots, celery, celery leaves and chilli, and pour in the hot water.

Bring to a boil, add the drained beans, reduce the heat, cover, and simmer for 1–2 hours until the beans are tender and the soup has thickened. Check frequently during cooking and add more hot water if necessary. The length of time to cook and the amount of additional water depends on the quality, age and condition of the beans.

Serve hot, sprinkled with freshly ground black pepper, and accompanied by olives, pickled vegetables and cheese.

Spanakorizo

Spinach with Rice

2 bunches of
English spinach

6 spring onions,
finely sliced

1 onion,
finely diced

1 cup of short-grain rice

1 cup of olive oil

lemon juice

3 tbsp fennel leaves

1 tsp salt

pepper

lemon wedge (to serve)

Wash your spinach thoroughly and chop it up roughly.

Put the spinach in a medium pan and steam. The spinach will wilt and release a lot of liquid. Drain but don't throw away the liquid.

Sauté the onions in a little olive oil.

Add the spinach, salt and pepper.

Wash the rice and sprinkle it on top of the spinach.

Now pour the reserved spinach liquid over the rice.

Close the lid and let the rice and spinach simmer for about 15-20 minutes.

Check the rice to ensure it has cooked.

Sprinkle the fennel leaves, lemon juice along with the olive oil on the rice. With a fork, tease the rice into the spinach. Serve with a wedge of lemon.

Fakes
Lentil Soup

500 g small red
or brown lentils

1 carrot, grated
or finely diced

2 celery stalks,
finely chopped

1 can of crushed tomatoes

1 large onion,
finely chopped

4 cloves of garlic,
peeled

6 tbsp olive oil
(plus more to serve)

6 tbsp red wine vinegar
(plus more to serve)

cold water

1 sprig of dried
oregano or rosemary

2 bay leaves

Lentils are a winter staple in Greece. This soup is served as a main meal, accompanied by olives, bread and cheese. It is gluten-free.

Fill a bowl with the vinegar. Crush one of the garlic cloves and add it to the bowl along with the oregano or rosemary sprig and one of the bay leaves. Leave aside for now.

Rinse the lentils then put them in a pot with 1¾ litres of cold water. Bring to a boil, turn off the heat, drain and throw this water out. Rinse the lentils.

Fill the pot with enough water to cover the lentils. Add the remaining garlic cloves and bay leaf, as well as the olive oil, onion, carrot and celery, and bring to a boil. Skim the surface of any white froth if necessary.

Once boiled, cover and simmer gently for about 25 minutes. Add the tomato, season well with salt and a little pepper, and simmer for a further 20 minutes or until the lentils are soft and the soup thickens. Take the lid off and simmer for another 5 minutes, longer if necessary, until the soup has a lovely thick consistency.

Take off the heat, splash in 3 tablespoons of the vinegar, and leave to stand for a few minutes before serving.

Serve hot with an extra drizzle of olive oil and with the remaining vinegar on the table for anyone who'd like more.

Lahanorizo
Cabbage with Rice

1 small cabbage

4 spring onions,
finely sliced

1 large onion,
finely diced

2 carrots, grated

1 zucchini, grated

2 sticks of celery,
finely sliced

1 cup of
medium-grain rice

½ cup of olive oil

juice of 2 lemons

1 cup of water

4 tbsp parsley,
finely chopped

1 tsp cooking salt

pepper, freshly ground

You can add ½ kilo
of minced meat to
this dish. The meat
will need to be sautéed
with the onion.

This is a dish that my dear father adored. He loved anything with cabbage. It is quick, easy to prepare, and makes for a great meal at any time.

Chop the cabbage roughly and blanch in hot water for about 5 minutes. Drain and set aside.

Sauté the onion in the olive oil until translucent. Add the spring onions, carrot, celery, zucchini and cabbage. Stir well and add the salt.

Cook well for another 10 minutes or so.

Add the rice along with a cup of water.

Close the lid and simmer until the rice has cooked. Turn off the stove.

Add the lemon juice and parsley. Stir and let it rest before serving.

Imam Baldi
Stuffed Eggplants

6-8 medium eggplants

3-4 ripe tomatoes,
roughly chopped

1 bunch of spring onions,
finely sliced

3 brown onions,
finely sliced

10 cloves of garlic,
finely sliced

1½ cups of olive oil

1 tbsp tomato paste

1 bunch of parsley,
washed and finely chopped

1 small bunch of mint,
finely chopped

salt

pepper

Believe me, once you have mastered this dish you will cook it again and again. It tastes even better the next day.

Preheat the oven to 180°C.

Cut the tops off the eggplants and slice down the middle lengthwise. Scoop out the flesh using a spoon. Take your time and be careful.

Finely chop up the flesh and sauté it in a pan with a little olive oil.

In a bowl, combine your chopped tomatoes, parsley, mint, onions, garlic, salt, pepper, tomato paste and half a cup of olive oil, creating a divine and aromatic mixture. Add the sautéed eggplant.

Lay the eggplant 'shells' in a baking dish. Spoon in the mixture until the shells are filled up.

Any remaining mixture should be spooned around the eggplant.

Drizzle over the remaining cup of olive oil and bake in an oven set to a moderate temperature for an hour. If the eggplants are browning too quickly, cover them with foil.

Gigantes

½ kg lima or butter beans

2 cups of celery,
finely chopped

1 medium carrot,
cut into cubes

1 small red capsicum,
sliced

1 can of crushed tomatoes

2 onions, finely sliced

2 cloves of garlic

1 tbsp tomato paste

2 bay leaves

a pinch of chilli flakes
(optional)

1 tsp sweet paprika

1 cup of parsley, chopped

1 tsp sugar

1 tsp salt

½ tsp pepper

I try wherever possible
to buy Australian beans.
Look for unblemished
white-coloured ones.
If they have a tinge
of yellow, they are
stale. In the event that
you cannot find the dried
variety, feel free to
use canned lima beans.
The recipe will be the
same except that you
do not have to bring
the beans to a boil.
Approximately 5 cans
will give you the
same quantity.

Gigantes translates as 'giant beans'. They are satisfying and healthy, and can be eaten immediately with crusty bread, olives and cheese. Alternatively, they can be left for a day to allow all the flavours to absorb. They are not only a favourite dish during Lent, but can also be enjoyed all year round.

Wash your beans thoroughly.

Fill a large saucepan with cold water and add your beans.

Bring the beans to a boil, simmer for 10 minutes then discard the water. Rinse the beans again.

In the same saucepan, add the beans and fill with cold water again. The water should be about 2 inches above the beans. Add the bay leaves, celery and carrot, then bring to a boil. Once bubbly, turn down your heat and simmer for 15-20 minutes.

In the meantime, sauté your onion and garlic in a deep frypan. Add the chilli flakes, tomato paste, crushed tomatoes, capsicum and paprika. Cook for 5 minutes.

Preheat the oven to 180°C. Using a ladle, pour the beans into a baking dish and then add the tomato mixture, salt, pepper and sugar. Mix carefully and thoroughly. The mixture should not be like a soup but it should not be dry either. Bake for 35 minutes, making sure the beans are cooked.

Sprinkle with parsley, noting that the amount of parsley depends on the quantity of the beans.

Mavromatika Fasolia Me Spanakia

Black-eyed Beans with Spinach

2 cups of
black-eyed beans

1 bunch of English
spinach (or baby spinach,
if preferred),
roughly chopped and
thoroughly washed

6 spring onions,
finely chopped

1 onion, sliced

1 cup of olive oil

1 tbsp white wine vinegar

juice of 1 lemon

a few sprigs of dill,
chopped

1 tsp cooking salt

pepper

crusty bread and feta
(to serve)

You can turn this into
a warm salad with grilled
chicken or steak.

*This dish can either be a salad or a main meal. The nuttiness
of the beans makes you want to eat more and more.
My youngest son, Jonathan, absolutely loves this meal.
He always says, 'Quality, Mum.'*

In a sieve, wash your beans thoroughly and then throw them into
a pan filled with cold water. Bring to a boil, drain and discard the
water. Rinse the beans again.

Fill the pot with cold water again and cook the beans for about
30 minutes. Always check them because they don't take long
and can easily become mushy.

In a shallow pan, sauté the onion in about half a cup of olive oil
until translucent. Add the spring onions, then the washed spinach,
salt and pepper.

Put the cooked beans in a bowl, add the wilted spinach and
mix using two forks so that you don't mush them up.

Add the lemon juice, vinegar and dill.

At this stage, add another half cup of olive oil.

Have a taste, and add more lemon juice if desired.

Serve with crusty bread and feta cheese.

FOR MY FAMILY,
PALM SUNDAY IS THE FIRST
DAY OF THE VERY IMPORTANT
EASTER HOLY WEEK.
THE TRADITIONAL MEAL
ON THIS DAY IS BAKALIARO:
COD THAT IS FRIED IN
BATTER AND SERVED WITH
SKORTHALIA (GARLIC DIP).

PALM SUNDAY

BAKALIARO
BEER-BATTERED SALTED COD

SKORTHALIA ME PATATES
SKORTHALIA WITH POTATOES

LAHANO SALATA
CABBAGE SALAD

Bakaliaro

Beer-battered Salted Cod

1-2 kg cod fillets
(dry salted cod can be
purchased at any major
Greek delicatessen)

sunflower oil (for
frying)

350 mL can of beer,
chilled

plain flour

a pinch of salt

---

*Cod and Palm Sunday are synonymous in my family. Mum would
prepare the cod on the Saturday, wake up early on Sunday,
fry it and then go to church.*

Start this recipe a day ahead.

Cut the cod into bite-sized pieces.

Place the pieces in a large non-reactive pot and fill it with
cold water so that the fish pieces are completely submerged.
You should do this at least 24 hours before frying your cod.

Change the water three to four times. This will release all the
excess salt and plump up the cod, which rehydrates.

Taste to check the saltiness of the fillets. If you are happy,
pour out the water and pat the pieces dry. If not, soak for a few
more hours.

To prepare the batter, pour the beer into a stainless-steel
bowl and, using chopsticks, mix in enough flour to make a batter
similar to pancake batter. Do not overwork it. Let the beer batter
sit in the fridge for up to 1 hour.

In a freezer bag, half filled with flour, add the cod fillets and shake
until coated.

Take your batter out of the fridge. Stir through some ice cubes.
The colder the batter is, the crispier the cod will turn out.

Fill a deep fry pan with sunflower oil to approximately two thirds
full. Heat the oil to the point where a cube of bread will brown in
20 seconds.

Dip your floured cod fillets into the batter and fry them
in the hot oil until golden. Do not overcrowd the pan. Take one
piece out and check to ensure the fish has cooked. If you find
that the fillets are becoming golden too quickly, reduce the
temperature of the oil.

Once cooked, drain the fillets on paper towels.

Arrange your fish on a platter. Serve it with skorthalia (garlic dip)
and a salad of your choice or horta (leafy green vegetables).

Skorthalia Me Patates
Skorthalia with Potatoes

500 g potatoes
(for boiling; I always
use Desiree potatoes)

4-6 cloves of garlic,
crushed

300-400 mL good-quality
olive oil

3 tbsp white wine vinegar

2 tbsp lemon juice

1½ tsp of cooking salt
(1 tsp for boiling and
an additional ½ tsp
when making potatoes)

½ tsp white pepper,
freshly ground

Make the skorthalia while
the potatoes are hot.

Skorthalia is best made in a mortar or a big bowl. Do not use a food processor, as this ruins the texture of the cooked potatoes by making them rubbery. A ricer is perfect for the potatoes.

Wash the potatoes thoroughly, leaving their skins on.

Fill a pot with water, add your potatoes and bring to a boil. Add a teaspoon of salt and cook until tender.

Drain and peel the potatoes when they are cool enough to handle.

Push the potatoes through a potato ricer into a large bowl.

Add the garlic, salt, pepper and vinegar.

While mixing thoroughly, gradually add the lemon juice and olive oil one after the other until your skorthalia is nice and thick.

Have a taste of the dip. If necessary, add more salt, lemon juice, vinegar or even garlic.

Lahano Salata

Cabbage Salad

½ white cabbage

¼ purple cabbage

2 carrots

½ cup of olive oil

juice of 1-2 lemons

1 small bunch of parsley

1 tsp cooking salt

Wash all the ingredients thoroughly.

Finely shred the cabbage.

Grate the carrots.

Finely chop the parsley.

In a big bowl, mix everything together (including the dressing made from the olive oil, lemon juice and salt).

Taste and add more salt or lemon juice if necessary.
I like it quite tangy.

EASTER

MAGIRITSA
GREEK EASTER LAMB SOUP

PLATI STO FOURNO
SLOW-ROASTED SHOULDER OF LAMB

DOLMATHAKIA
DOLMADES

KOUNOPITHY SALATA
CAULIFLOWER SALAD

PATSARIA SALATA
BEETROOT SALAD

POTATOES WITH TOMATOES, GARLIC AND ONION

RED DYED EASTER EGGS

THIPLES

For Greeks, religious customs are alive and Christmas,
Easter and the Assumption of the Virgin Mary (15 August)
are considered to be the greatest of religious feasts.
Of these three, Easter is by far the most important.

In Greece, Easter takes place in spring and so many
of the customs and traditions are tied to the arrival
of spring. The Easter Egg, for instance, represents life,
heaven, earth and fertility.

Easter Holy Week is the most important time in the Greek
Orthodox calendar. During Holy Week, Orthodox churches
conduct services every evening. Good Friday is a
particularly special service, as a flowered tomb of the
Christ (Epitaphios) symbolically takes its place as the
focal point of the service. Not only do we go to church
every night of this week, fast and prepare ourselves
for communion, but as with every traditional Greek
household, spare time is spent baking sweet treats.
All houses are busy baking Koulourakia, making
Melomakarona and Tsoureki (traditional Greek Easter
sweet bread), and dyeing eggs. On the Saturday,
we go from house to house exchanging our treats.
We all take such pride in our efforts.

I love Easter. There is something soothing,
reassuring and quite comforting about this important
week. It is a time for reflecting and appreciating all
that is important in our lives: family, tradition and
the joy of celebrating the resurrection of Christ.

Magiritsa

Greek Easter Lamb Soup

2 lamb shanks

3 lamb necks

2 sticks of celery,
cut into pieces

2 heads of baby
cos lettuce

1 whole bunch
of spring onions,
finely sliced

1 onion

5-6 cloves of garlic

½ cup of
medium-grain rice

3 eggs

olive oil

juice of 2 lemons

8 cups of chicken stock

approx. 2 L water,
plus more for boiling

1 cup of parsley,
finely chopped

2 tbsp dill,
finely chopped

1 tsp salt

10 peppercorns

You will also need
a hand-held electric
beater.

In Greece, Easter comes at the heart of springtime, when lambs are in season. After the 40-day Lent period, Greek families break their fast with this delectable soup called Magiritsa. Traditionally it is eaten after the midnight mass and is made using leftover parts of the lamb.

In my family, however, we make this soup using lamb shanks and necks.

Put the lamb shanks and necks in a pot of cold water. Bring to a boil and simmer for 5 minutes. Discard this water. Wash all the meat thoroughly.

Fill your pot up again with 2 litres of cold water. Add the celery sticks, onion, peppercorns, garlic and salt, followed by the meat. Simmer for 2–3 hours, until the lamb is 'fork-tender'.

Take all the meat out of the broth and place on a plate. Cover with cling wrap.

In another pot, sauté the spring onions in a little olive oil. Add in the broth with the vegetables and combine with chicken stock.

Taste to see whether the broth needs more salt or pepper. Add a little more seasoning if necessary.

Clear all the meat off the bones and return these pieces to the broth.

Wash and roughly chop the cos lettuce, then add it to the broth.

Add the parsley, dill and rice and simmer gently for about 30–45 minutes.

To make the egg-lemon sauce, beat the egg whites using a hand-held electric beater until soft peaks form. Add the egg yolks and continue beating.

Pour in the lemon juice, then gently ladle in some hot stock. Continue beating for a minute or two.

Pour the egg-lemon sauce into the pot of broth and stir to bring all the ingredients together.

You need to taste again to see if the salt-to-lemon ratio is to your liking. Adjust accordingly. The soup should be slightly tangy.

Enjoy and, as we say at Easter time, 'Xristos Anesti!' – 'Christ has risen!'

Plati Sto Fourno
Slow-roasted Shoulder of Lamb

1 shoulder of lamb

2 lemons, skin and pith removed so you have just the flesh

3 onions

1 head of garlic

8 cloves of garlic, peeled and sliced in half

olive oil

1 tbsp oregano

sprigs of rosemary

2 tsp cooking salt

1 tsp black pepper

Start with the best lamb. I buy Salt Bush lamb from my butcher and get him to de-bone it, leaving only the shank. You can leave the bones if you prefer.

Select your best platter and serve your friends and family a dish that they will never forget!

Slow-roasted Shoulder of Lamb is a family favourite. It is the hero dish we make on Easter Sunday. The aromas of the lamb, garlic, lemon and herbs permeate the kitchen as it slowly cooks. After the long period of fasting from any meat product, we await anxiously to sit at the table to enjoy the succulent lamb. That said, I do cook this dish at other times throughout the year as well, especially if I'm entertaining for lunch or dinner.

Firstly, clean your lamb using a damp paper towel. Remove any fat that you don't want, but don't remove too much because fat keeps the meat moist.

Preheat your oven to 200°C.

Clean and peel the onions. Slice them about ¼ inch thick and assemble them on the bottom of the baking dish. Sprinkle a little salt and pepper on them and drizzle olive oil.

Place the lamb on top.

In a bowl, put the salt, pepper and oregano. Generously sprinkle the seasoning over the lamb on both sides.

Using a sharp knife, make incisions all over the lamb. Insert the garlic cloves and a little rosemary into these incisions.

Now you need to slice your lemons and place the slices all over the lamb.

Cut the whole head of garlic in half and place halves in the baking dish.

Drizzle a little olive oil over the top of the lamb.

Tear a sheet of baking paper large enough to cover your dish. Wet it under a tap, scrunch it up and cover your lamb as though the baking paper were a little blanket.

Cover the entire baking dish with foil and put it in the oven. For the first 30 minutes, bake it at 200°C in a fan-forced oven. Then reduce your temperature to 150°C and bake for a further 1½ hours.

Remove the foil and baking paper and bake the lamb uncovered for another 30 minutes.

Dolmathakia

Dolmades

500 g grape (vine)
leaves, fresh or
preserved in brine

2 cups (175 g)
of shallots and
spring onions,
finely chopped

2 large onions, chopped

2½ cups (500 g)
of medium-grain rice

4 tbsp pine nuts, toasted

2 cups (450 mL)
of olive oil

5 tbsp lemon juice,
freshly squeezed

2½ cups (600 mL)
of boiling water

½ cup (15 g)
of fresh dill, chopped

½ cup of parsley, chopped

salt

pepper

tzatziki or plain yoghurt
(to serve)

The parsley can be
replaced with chopped
fresh mint and the
dill with chopped
fennel fronds.

Vine leaves can be
bought in a jar or
vacuum-packed as well.

Dolmades are vine leaves stuffed with rice and herbs. They can be served as a mezze, snack or light meal, and are great with tzatziki or feta cheese. They are gluten-free.

Rinse the vine leaves and trim off the stems if necessary.

Bring a pan of water to a boil, add the leaves a few at a time, and blanch briefly. Drain and let cool. (This step is necessary only if you are using fresh vine lives.)

Spread out some of the leaves to cover the base of a large, wide, heavy pan. Alternatively, slice an onion into rings and put the rings at the bottom of the saucepan.

Put the shallots and spring onions into a colander, sprinkle with a little salt, and rub with your fingers. Rinse them with a little water, then drain by squeezing out as much liquid as possible.

Combine the rice, shallots, spring onions, herbs, half the oil, pine nuts and a squeeze of lemon juice in a bowl, and season with salt and pepper.

Lay a leaf out flat on the work surface, shiny side down. Put about one tablespoon of the rice mixture at the stem end in the middle, fold the sides over the filling, and loosely roll up into a neat parcel. Continue making vine leaf parcels until all the ingredients have been used.

Arrange the stuffed leaves in the lined pan, side by side, seam side down. (You may have to make more than one layer.)

Carefully pour the remaining oil, boiling water and lemon juice into the pan. Invert a heavy plate on the top of the parcels to prevent them from opening during cooking.

Cover the pan and bring to a boil, then reduce the heat and simmer for 35–40 minutes until all the water has been absorbed.

Remove from the heat. Place a cotton towel or some paper towels between the pan and the lid to absorb the steam, and let cool.

Transfer the Dolmades to a serving platter and serve with tzatziki or plain yoghurt. They are just as good served cold the next day.

Kounopithy Salata
Cauliflower Salad

1 cauliflower

1 pomegranate

4 tbsp olive oil

juice of 1-2 lemons

½ cup of cracked wheat,
soaked in hot water for
about an hour and drained

1 bunch flat-leaf
parsley, chopped

½ tsp salt

cracked pepper

This is a wonderful
salad that can be
served with chicken,
fish or meat.

Wash the cauliflower thoroughly then steam it until it is soft.

Once cooked, place the cauliflower into a bowl and, while still hot, chop it up into small florets. Pour in the olive oil, lemon juice, parsley, salt and pepper as well as the cracked wheat that has been soaked and drained. Stir to blend all the ingredients together.

Taste to see whether it needs more salt or lemon juice and adjust accordingly. The salad should be slightly tangy.

Once you are happy with the flavour, tap in the pomegranate seeds using a wooden spoon.

Patsaria Salata

Beetroot Salad

1 bunch of beetroot
(preferably not the
baby ones; large beetroots
are more appropriate
for this recipe —
look for ones with fresh,
bright green leaves)

2 cloves of garlic,
thinly sliced

1 cup of olive oil

½ cup of red wine vinegar

1 cup of water

1 level tsp salt

feta (to serve)

Preheat the oven to 180°C.

Cut the stem and the leaves off the beetroot bulbs. Set stems and leaves aside.

Wash the bulbs thoroughly. Line a baking tray with foil and place the beetroots on top.

Drizzle them with olive oil and add a cup of water so the beetroots do not dry out.

Roast them in the oven on moderate heat for approximately 45 minutes.

Remove the bulbs from the oven and test them. If a skewer goes through, they're ready.

In the meantime, cut the stems into 2-inch lengths and together with the leaves, steam them until tender.

In a big bowl, slice the beetroots. I like to cut them into wedges. Add the stems and leaves. Add the olive oil, salt, vinegar and garlic. Taste and add more salt or vinegar if necessary.

Serve sprinkled with feta cheese on top.

Potatoes with Tomatoes, Garlic and Onion

1.2 kg potatoes,
peeled and rinsed

2 ripe tomatoes,
cut into chunks

1 red onion, sliced

6 cloves of garlic

6 tbsp olive oil

500 mL water

1 heaped tsp
dried oregano

1 tbsp sweet paprika

1 bay leaf

salt

pepper

You will also need
a 22 × 30 cm ovenproof
dish.

This is a very versatile potato dish. You can serve it as a meal or as an accompaniment to chicken or meat.

Preheat the oven to 180°C.

Halve the potatoes lengthwise then cut each half into two or three gondolas, depending on the size or your potatoes. Spread them in an ovenproof dish. Scatter the tomato and onion over the potatoes, and generously drizzle the olive oil, salt and pepper. Crush the oregano between your fingers, letting it fall over the potatoes, and add the paprika, garlic and bay leaf as well.

Turn the potatoes to coat them well with everything. Dribble the water down the sides of the dish and shuffle it.

Roast the potatoes for about 1 ½ hours until they are tender and the sauce is thick. Turn and baste the potatoes every 20 minutes or so, and make sure that nothing is sticking to the bottom of the dish. Also check that the potatoes are not out of the liquid for too long.

Taste to see if the potatoes need any more salt and pepper. Serve hot.

Red Dyed Easter Eggs

2 dozen small
to medium white eggs

2 packets of
Greek red egg dye

1 cup of sunflower oil

2 cups of vinegar

water

a variety of herbs
(any pretty leaf you'd
like to see on your eggs,
such as parsley, dill,
even leaves from flowers)

You will also need a wide
cooking pot, stockings,
a cloth, string and a few
old newspapers.

Easter is a time to celebrate that we had prepared ourselves through Lent, cleaning, reflecting and praying. During Holy Week, we go to church every night and during the day all the women bake traditional festive sweets. It is on Easter Thursday that we dye the eggs. Their red colouring symbolises the blood of Christ.

Start working the night before. Firstly, have your eggs at room temperature. Wash and dry them thoroughly. Check for any cracks and get rid of eggs that are damaged.

Prepare your leaves. Using a wet sponge, moisten your leaves and attach them to the egg. Get a piece of stocking, cover the egg with it and, using some string, tie a knot at both ends. It will look like a bon-bon. Make sure they are secured firmly to prevent the leaves from moving.

The next day, Easter Thursday, prepare your dye according to the packet's instructions. The only difference is that for two dozen eggs I add two cups of vinegar. I find that this assists in achieving a more intense colour.

To begin cooking, submerge a sheet of newspaper on the bottom of the cooking pot. Put a single layer of eggs on the newspaper then cover with another layer of newspaper. Continue until all the eggs are in the pot. Cover with a final layer of newspaper. The newspaper cushions the eggs, preventing cracking. Simmer for a little longer than a normal hard-boiled egg (about 10 minutes).

Remove the eggs from the heat and let them stand in the dye for several more minutes before taking them out.

Using a cloth dampened with oil, start wiping and polishing your eggs after removing the stockings. The oil helps to remove the leaves and makes your eggs shine. Display them on a beautiful platter.

Thiples

Pastry

16 eggs
(for the best results,
they must be fresh
and organic)

approx. 2 kg special
white flour

1 L sunflower oil

juice of ½ lemon

½ cup of ouzo

25 g packet of
vanilla sugar

2½ tbsp sugar

3 cups of walnuts
(to serve)

1 cup of sesame seeds,
toasted (to serve)

1 tsp of cinnamon
(to serve)

Syrup

2 cups of honey

½ cup of lemon juice

1 cup of water

1 stick of cinnamon

2 cups of sugar

Thiples are a traditional pastry made for all festive occasions such as weddings, christenings, birthdays, Name Days and so on. They are light, crunchy and deliciously sweet. Thiples are not traditionally made in Thessaly, where my parents come from, and I learned how to make them through my mother-in-law, Anastasia, who comes from Kalamata.

In a large bowl, beat the eggs, sugar, vanilla sugar, lemon juice and ouzo.

Add the flour to form a stiff dough. It should not stick to your hands. Knead it for about 5 minutes and allow it to rest for about 30–50 minutes.

Take a piece of dough the size of your fist and, using a pasta machine, roll the dough out until it is thin. Cut your pastry into squares approximately 6 by 6 inches in size.

Heat the oil in a deep frying pan. Drop the pastry squares into the hot oil and, using a large fork, roll them up to form a cylinder. Admittedly, this step does require a bit of practice. Don't worry if they are not perfect to begin with. Drain the Thiples after frying.

Create the syrup by bringing all the syrup ingredients to a boil and simmer for about 5–10 minutes.

Dip each of the Thiples into the warm (not hot) syrup.

Serve on a beautiful platter and sprinkle with the finely chopped walnuts, sesame seeds and a little cinnamon.

EVERYDAY FAMILY FEAST

KOKKINISTO KREAS
SLOW-COOKED BEEF CASSEROLE

PILAF

PAPOUTSAKIA WITH WHITE SAUCE

CABBAGE ROLLS

EVERY DAY IS A CAUSE FOR CELEBRATION
AS WE GIVE THANKS FOR FAMILY,
FRIENDS AND HEALTH. EVERY MEAL IS A FEAST.
THE GREEK HABIT OF SHARING A DINNER
TABLE WITH FRIENDS AT HOME IS DEEPLY
ROOTED IN OUR SOCIAL PRACTICES.
IT IS NEVER ABOUT THE FOOD ITSELF
BUT RATHER THE ABILITY TO SHARE THE
SIMPLEST INGREDIENTS AROUND THE TABLE
AS WE CELEBRATE LIFE.

Kokkinisto Kreas
Slow-cooked Beef Casserole

1½ kg round steak,
cleaned and cut
into cubes

3 cans of roma tomatoes,
crushed by hand

1 onion, finely diced

2-3 cloves of garlic

½ cup of olive oil,
plus an additional 2 tbsp

1 tbsp red wine vinegar

1 L water or
chicken stock

1 tbsp tomato paste

1 tsp sweet paprika

a pinch of cinnamon

a few basil leaves

1 bay leaf

1 tsp sugar

1 tsp cooking salt

1 tsp pepper

This is a delicious
family meal. It can
be served with pilaf
and a dollop of yoghurt
on top. Alternatively,
mashed potatoes are
also delicious with
this casserole.

If you want to take
this casserole further,
you can also add peas
and carrots.

*Kokkinisto Kreas is a delicious, all-year-round dish made with
lean beef, tomatoes and a hint of cinnamon, and slow-cooked
for 1–1½ hours. Rice, pasta or mashed potatoes can all
be served as accompaniments, and chicken or lamb can
be used instead of beef.*

*Kokkinisto Kreas served with pilaf reminds me of my sons
growing up — in particular, my eldest son. Simon absolutely loves
this meal. Whenever I would prepare it he would wait anxiously
and devour the whole plate without any argument.*

In a heavy-based wide casserole dish, brown your meat a little
at a time so that it doesn't stew.

Once all the meat has browned, add the onion and the garlic cloves.
Stir a few times.

Add the tomato paste and sweet paprika, and cook for
a few minutes.

Add the canned tomatoes, sugar, salt, pepper, cinnamon and
bay leaf as well as the half cup of olive oil.

Add 1 litre of water or chicken stock if you like, close the lid,
and simmer gently for about 1 hour. Check every so often and stir.

The liquid will evaporate, leaving a lusciously thick tomato sauce.
The meat should be soft and melt in your mouth. If the meat
needs more cooking, just add a little more water and continue
to simmer. In the final 15 minutes, add the 2 tablespoons of oil,
basil leaves and red wine vinegar.

Pilaf

1½ cups of basmati rice
or long-grain rice

½ cup of olive oil

3 cups of hot
chicken stock
(see 'Chicken Stock'
recipe on page 234)

1 tsp cooking salt

I like to use little
moulds to serve the
pilaf. Even a teacup
will suffice.

Pilaf is a rice dish that should be mastered because it is an excellent accompaniment to many Greek dishes including Kokkinisto Kreas, Keftethes Me Saltsa and so many more.

Start off with an excellent homemade chicken stock. Commercially bought stock will be okay if you don't have the homemade variety.

Wash your rice thoroughly.

Using a pan with a lid, heat the oil then add the rice. Toast gently. Add the salt and continue to stir.

Add the chicken stock. Be careful as the hot stock will bubble profusely. Put the lid on and simmer until you see little pockets of holes on the surface of the rice. Turn off the stove. Lift the lid, place a clean tea towel on top of the rice, then fit the lid on. Leave for about 10–15 minutes.

Take the lid and tea towel away. Using a fork, fluff up your rice and serve.

Papoutsakia
with White Sauce

4 eggplants,
halved lengthwise

500 g canned or fresh
tomatoes, peeled,
seeded and chopped

500 g minced beef

3 spring onions,
finely sliced

1 onion, grated

4 cloves of garlic

1 cup (120 g)
of grated kefalotiri*

1 cup of breadcrumbs

1 egg white

1 cup (250 mL)
of olive oil

1½ cups (350 mL)
of white sauce
(see 'Béchamel Sauce'
recipe on page 234)

1 tbsp tomato paste

½ cup (120 mL)
of hot water

1 tbsp allspice, ground

½ cup (25 g) fresh
parsley, finely chopped

salt

pepper

*Kefalotiri is a hard
cheese that Greeks
use for cooking;
it tastes delicious.

Make two or three slashes in the flesh of each piece of eggplant using a knife, taking care not to cut through the outer skin. Sprinkle liberally with salt, and let drain in a colander for 1-2 hours. Rinse under cold running water, squeeze out any excess moisture and pat dry.

Heat half the oil in a skillet or frying pan. Add the eggplants and cook over medium heat, turning occasionally, for 6-8 minutes until lightly browned, then remove from the frypan and drain on paper towels. Put them in an ovenproof earthenware dish, side by side and flesh side up.

Heat the remaining oil in a pan. Add the spring onions, onion, garlic, tomatoes and tomato paste, and cook over low heat, stirring occasionally, for 5 minutes until softened.

Stir in the minced beef and cook, stirring and breaking up the meat with the spoon, for about 10 minutes until the sauce has reduced. Mix in the allspice. Add the water and simmer for 20 minutes. Remove from the heat and let cool.

Preheat the oven to 180°C. Lightly beat the egg white and stir it into the meat mixture. Using a spoon, carefully scoop out the flesh from the eggplants. Chop up this flesh roughly and mix it into the meat mixture. Add parsley and spoon this mixture into the eggplant halves.

Add half the grated cheese into the white sauce and spread the sauce evenly over the stuffed eggplants. Sprinkle with the remaining cheese, and season with pepper.

Sprinkle a generous amount of breadcrumbs over the bottom of the baking dish. Line up the eggplant halves and bake for about 45-60 minutes.

Cabbage Rolls

1 whole cabbage
(the savoy variety is
usually easier because
the leaves are softer
when blanched)

1 kg minced meat
(a mixture of beef
and pork is tastiest)

a small bunch of spring
onions, finely sliced

3 onions, finely chopped

2 cups of calrose rice
(short-grain)

1 tbsp cornflour

3 eggs

1 cup of olive oil

2 cups of hot chicken
stock or water

juice of 1 lemon

½ tsp of cumin powder

a small bunch of dill,
finely chopped

a small bunch of parsley,
finely chopped

salt

pepper

This dish can be finished
off with tomato sauce
instead of egg-lemon
sauce. To do this,
crush one can's worth
of tomatoes into the
stock and pour over the
rolls before cooking.

Select a good cabbage that is not too firm. Cut the core out from the centre and then blanch in a big pot of salted boiling water for about 10–15 minutes. The hole should face the bottom of the pot. Take out the cabbage carefully and let it cool a little.

Once the cabbage has cooled, start unwrapping it slowly and carefully and place the leaves into a big dish where they can't be damaged.

Soak the rice in cold water for 10 minutes, then drain and rinse.

Prepare the stuffing by combining the minced meat, lemon juice, rice, onions, spring onions, one egg, cumin and fresh herbs in a bowl. Mix in half the olive oil and a teaspoon of salt and pepper.

Cut the larger leaves of the cabbage in half and trim off any hard cores. Place about 1 tablespoon of your stuffing at one end of the leaf and fold the end of the leaf over so it looks like a short, fat cigar. Then fold in the sides and roll up fairly tightly to make a neat package ('dolmathes').

Line a large, wide, heavy pan with any leaves that you haven't used. Onion slices will also work well. Layer the dolmathes in the pan, packing them tightly together. Season each layer as you go along. If you have a lot of dolmathes, it's a good idea to use two pans to ensure that they don't overcook.

Drizzle the remaining olive oil over the top of the dolmathes.

Invert a small, heatproof plate on top of the last layer of dolmathes. Pour in enough hot chicken stock or water to just cover the top layer. Cover and simmer gently for about 45 minutes. As soon as the dolmathes are cooked, tilt the pan, holding the plate down firmly, and empty most of the liquid into a bowl. Let the liquid cool slightly.

To make the egg-lemon sauce, mix the cornflour with a little water to create a paste. Whisk the rest of the eggs in another bowl, then add to this the lemon juice and the cornflour mixture. Whisk again. Continue to whisk, gradually adding tablespoons of the slightly cooled cooking liquid from the dolmathes. As soon as all of the liquid has been added, pour the sauce over the dolmathes and gently shake the pan to distribute the sauce evenly.

Cook for a further 3–5 minutes until the sauce thickens, rotating the saucepan gently.

PETER'S NAME DAY
15 AUGUST

MOUSSAKA

SALATA ME FASOLIA
LIMA BEAN SALAD

YIOUVARELAKIA

OKTAPODI STI SKARA
CHARGRILLED OCTOPUS

IN GREECE THE FEAST OF THE
DORMITION [ASSUMPTION]
OF THE VIRGIN MARY — WHO IS ALSO
KNOWN BY THE NAME PANAGIA —
IS A PUBLIC HOLIDAY.
HERE IN AUSTRALIA, ALL GREEKS
CONTINUE THE TRADITION
BY HAVING PARISH CELEBRATIONS
AND VISITING EACH OTHER'S HOMES.
ON THIS DAY, WE ALSO CELEBRATE
MY HUSBAND'S NAME DAY.
HIS GREEK NAME IS PANAGIOTIS
[WHICH TRANSLATES TO PETER],
IN HONOUR OF PANAGIA.

BEING GREEK MEANS THAT
WE ARE ALWAYS CELEBRATING
AROUND A TABLE.
FAMILY AND FRIENDS ARE THE
CORNERSTONES OF MY LIFE.

Moussaka

1 kg lean minced beef

2 kg eggplants, cut into 1 cm slices

2 cups (450 mL) of peeled fresh or canned tomatoes, pureed

1 onion, grated

2 cloves of garlic, sliced

5 tbsp fine dried breadcrumbs

1 cup (100 g) of kefalotiri

5 tbsp heavy (double) cream

3 cups (750 mL) of béchamel sauce (see recipe on page 234)

1 egg white, lightly beaten

½ cup (120 mL) of olive oil

¼ tsp allspice, ground

½ bunch parsley, finely chopped

½ tsp sugar

salt

pepper

You will also need a 25 × 35 cm ovenproof dish.

You can replace half or all the eggplants with sliced potatoes or zucchini. If using potatoes, line the base of the dish with them so they can absorb the juices.

Moussaka is a traditional dish eaten all over Greece. It features layers of eggplant and minced meat, topped with a creamy béchamel sauce, and is baked in the oven. Moussaka is best served with fresh bread and salad.

Sprinkle the eggplant slices with salt and let drain in a colander for 1 hour. Rinse, squeeze out the excess water and pat dry. Heat half the oil in a skillet or frying pan. Add the eggplants and cook over medium heat, turning occasionally, for 6-8 minutes until lightly browned on both sides. Remove with a slotted spoon and drain on paper towels. You can also grill your eggplants.

Heat the remaining oil in a heavy pan. Add the onion and garlic and cook over low heat, stirring occasionally, for 5 minutes until softened. Increase the heat to medium, add the minced beef and cook, stirring and breaking it up with the spoon, for 10 minutes, until lightly browned. Add the tomatoes, allspice and sugar, and season with salt and pepper. Reduce the heat and simmer for 15-20 minutes or until all the liquid has evaporated.

Remove from the heat and let cool, then fold in the egg white and parsley.

Preheat the oven to 200°C. Grease the ovenproof dish with oil and sprinkle it with 2 tablespoons of the breadcrumbs, forming a thin layer on the bottom.

Cover the base of the dish with half the prepared eggplant slices, overlapping them slightly.

Spread half the meat mixture on top, then sprinkle with half the grated cheese and 2 tablespoons of the remaining breadcrumbs.

Cover the meat and cheese with the remaining eggplant slices, spread the remaining meat mixture on top, and sprinkle with the rest of the breadcrumbs. (At this point, the dish can be covered and frozen. Thaw before baking.)

Stir the cream into the béchamel sauce and spread it evenly over the surface of the dish.

Bake for about 50 minutes or until the top is golden brown. Remove from the oven and let stand for 15 minutes before serving.

Salata Me Fasolia

Lima Bean Salad

3 cans of lima
(butter) beans

1 can of chickpeas

1 red capsicum,
finely diced

½ bunch of spring onions,
finely sliced

1 red onion,
thinly sliced

½ cup of olive oil

juice of 2 lemons

1 bunch of parsley,
finely chopped

1 tsp salt

Lima Bean Salad is one of my favourites. It tastes delicious, is colourful and very good for you. I make it at the Sweet Greek shop and always run out. The other great thing about the salad is that you can use canned lima (butter) beans.

Salata Me Fasolia can be eaten as a meal on its own. Alternatively, add tuna to this salad or serve it as a side to meat, fish or chicken.

Drain all the beans and rinse thoroughly.

In a big bowl, mix them well with the onions, parsley, capsicum, spring onions, salt, lemon juice and olive oil.

Let the salad stand for half an hour to allow the flavours to merge. Stir again and taste to see whether it needs more olive oil, lemon juice or salt.

Yiouvarelakia

1 kg minced beef

2 small onions,
finely grated

1 cup of rice

4 eggs (3 for the
egg-lemon sauce)

4 tbsp olive oil
(2 to go into the
stock or water)

4 tbsp lemon juice,
freshly squeezed

5 cups (1.2 L) of
beef stock or water

3 tbsp parsley,
finely chopped

¼ tsp allspice

1 tsp salt

pepper, freshly ground

You will need a hand-held
electric beater.

Combine the minced beef, 1 egg, onion, rice, herbs and olive oil
in a large bowl, and season with allspice, salt and pepper.
Knead briefly and refrigerate for an hour.

Roll the beef mixture into small balls. Set aside.

Pour the stock or water into a large pan. Add the oil, season with
salt and pepper, and bring to a boil.

Add the meatballs a few at a time to avoid lowering the temperature.
Reduce the heat, cover, and simmer the Yiouvarelakia for about
30 minutes, or until the meat and rice are cooked.

Meanwhile, separate the 3 remaining eggs and beat the whites to
soft peaks.

Beat in the yolks then add the lemon juice. Beat in a ladleful of the
hot stock, then gradually stir the mixture back into the soup.
Immediately remove the pan from the heat and serve
the soup sprinkled with freshly ground pepper.

Oktapodi Sti Skara

Chargrilled Octopus

1 octopus, cleaned
(thawed if you are buying
it frozen)

1 onion, sliced

3-4 cloves of garlic

rind of 1 lemon

½ cup of red wine vinegar

lemon juice (to serve)

oregano (to serve)

salt and pepper
(to serve)

Chargrilled Octopus reminds me of Greek taverns, whether here or in Greece. Visualise the octopus on a platter sprinkled with oregano, drizzled with olive oil and a squeeze of lemon juice, with a bottle of ouzo, crusty bread and the water lapping at your feet.

It really is so easy to master Chargrilled Octopus. The main factors are to buy cleaned octopus from your fishmonger, and to simmer it first in a saucepan before placing it on a grill platter or barbecue.

Combine the lemon rind, onion, garlic and red wine vinegar in a pot with the octopus. Make sure the pot is non-reactive — a stainless-steel pot will be perfect.

The octopus will release some liquid. Simmer it gently until it is tender and has a pinky, purple colour.

Allow the octopus to cool in the pan with its juices.

Once the octopus has cooled down, it is ready to be grilled. A hot chargrill fire will give the best end result in terms of flavour. If this is not possible, a gas barbecue will be fine.

Rub olive oil all over the tentacles and grill, turning over once. Once the octopus has been grilled, cut it into 1-inch pieces.

Drizzle the chargrilled octopus pieces with olive oil, lemon juice, salt, pepper, oregano and slices of garlic. Stir well, and add salt and lemon juice according to your taste — the octopus should taste lemony. Serve it with a glass of ouzo on ice.

WINTER IS A TIME FOR HOT,
HEARTY COMFORT FOOD
THAT NOURISHES THE SOUL.
I LIKE TO STAY IN THE WARMTH
OF MY KITCHEN AND PREPARE THESE
SLOW-COOKED MEALS.

HEARTY WINTER MEALS

YIOUVETSI

TSOUTZOUKAKIA IN TOMATO SAUCE
MEAT RISSOLES IN TOMATO SAUCE

KOUNELI STIFATHO
RABBIT CASSEROLE WITH BABY ONIONS

KOTA AVGOLEMONO
CHICKEN SOUP WITH EGG-LEMON SAUCE

FRIKASSE HIRINO
ME SELINO AVGOLEMONO
PORK CASSEROLE WITH CELERY

Yiouvetsi

1½ kg beef or
lamb fillets, diced

1 can of tomatoes,
crushed

1 onion, finely diced

500 g packet of
kritharaki (orzo)

1 cup of kefalotiri,
grated

½ cup of olive oil

4-5 cups of water
or stock

1 tbsp tomato paste

salt

pepper

Yiouvetsi can be made with beef, lamb or chicken; the process remains the same. You can even use a whole chicken or chicken thighs, which I find easier and tastier. It's hearty and comforting and, during winter, should be enjoyed regularly. Cook it for your family and friends. Use a different meat each time to develop your own favourite rendition of the dish.

Brown your meat in a large saucepan. Do this slowly so as to not overcrowd your saucepan.

Once the meat pieces have browned, tip them into a baking dish and keep warm. Add the onions and sauté until translucent, then add the tomatoes and tomato paste.

Tip your meat back into the saucepan and add the water or stock. Bring to a boil and simmer for about 30 minutes.

Preheat your oven to 180°C. Pour the meat with all the liquid into the baking dish, add a little more liquid if necessary, and bake for a further 30-45 minutes until the meat is tender.

At this stage, pour the orzo into the baking dish, give it a stir, and add salt and pepper. Bake covered for about 10 minutes until the orzo has cooked. Ensure that there is enough liquid for the orzo.

Take out of the oven, grate the kefalotiri cheese on top and serve hot.

Tsoutzoukakia in Tomato Sauce

Meat Rissoles in Tomato Sauce

1½ kg minced lamb and beef

2 cans of tomatoes, crushed by hand

2 onions, very finely chopped or grated

2 cloves of garlic, finely grated

100 g fresh breadcrumbs

1 egg, beaten

4 tbsp olive oil, plus 100 mL for the tomato sauce

250 mL chicken stock

1 tbsp tomato paste

a pinch of chilli flakes

a good bunch of parsley, finely chopped

1 tsp cumin, ground

a pinch of cinnamon

a pinch of allspice

1 tsp sugar

salt

pepper

You can crumble some feta cheese on top of your dish — absolutely scrumptious!

Tsoutzoukakia are cumin-flavoured, sausage-shaped rissoles. We owe their popularity to the Greeks who once lived in Smyrna (now Izmir) in Turkey. The rissoles are best served with rice, pasta or Greek salad.

To make the Tsoutzoukakia, combine the minced meat, breadcrumbs, onion, half of the garlic, parsley, cumin, cinnamon, allspice, salt and pepper in a bowl.

Stir in the beaten egg then knead the mixture for about 5 minutes until the mixture forms a paste. Leave in the fridge for about an hour.

Meanwhile, prepare the tomato sauce. Mix the tomatoes, tomato paste, chicken stock, sugar, 100 mL of olive oil, remaining garlic, chilli flakes, salt and pepper into a large saucepan with a wide base. Bring to a boil then simmer for about 30 minutes.

With dampened hands, take the meat mixture and form sausage shapes about 9 centimetres long. Fry them in the remaining olive oil until brown on all sides.

Using a slotted spoon, transfer the sausages to the saucepan containing the tomato sauce and simmer for 10-15 minutes. Allow them to rest for about 30 minutes. Serve on a beautiful platter.

Kouneli Stifatho

Rabbit Casserole with Baby Onions

1 whole rabbit,
cut into portions

1 kg baby pickling
onions, peeled and left
whole

1 whole head of garlic,
peeled

1 cup of olive oil

1 glass of red wine

2 tbsp red wine vinegar

2 tbsp tomato paste,
diluted in a little water

3 bay leaves

a pinch of chilli flakes

1 stick of cinnamon

4-5 allspice berries

1 tbsp sugar

1 tsp cooking salt

pepper, freshly ground

Enjoy this rich dish on
a bed of mashed potatoes
or simply with bread.

*This is an amazing dish. You will discover many layers of flavour —
from sweet to savoury, spicy to aromatic. My dad would yearn
for my mother's rendition of this dish. He really didn't care whether
it was rabbit or beef so long as she cooked it.*

Start this recipe a day ahead.

In a shallow baking dish, combine the red wine, red wine vinegar,
bay leaves and allspice berries. Marinate the rabbit pieces
in this mixture overnight, turning over every chance you get.

The next day, take the rabbit pieces out. Pat dry and set the
marinade aside.

In a shallow non-stick pan, gently brown the rabbit pieces
and place them in a baking dish.

Preheat the oven to 175°C.

In another pan, heat the oil. Add the pickling onions, which have
been peeled and left whole, and gently brown them. Add the
sugar to the pan and allow to caramelise.

Assemble the onions all around the rabbit pieces in the
baking dish. Pour in the marinade, and add the cinnamon stick,
bay leaves, tomato paste, salt, pepper and garlic.

Cover and bake in the oven for at least an hour.

Take the baking dish out. Check the rabbit pieces to ensure they
have cooked. If they have and a large amount of marinate remains,
cook on the stove for a short while to reduce the liquid.
You should have a glossy, syrupy sauce.

Kota Avgolemono

Chicken Soup with Egg-lemon Sauce

1 organic or
free-range chicken

1 stick of celery,
chopped

2 onions, chopped

1½ cups of
medium-grain rice

1 tbsp cornflour

3 eggs (at room
temperature)

juice of 1-2 lemons

2½ L water

1 bay leaf

1 tsp salt

5-6 peppercorns

You will also need
a hand-held electric
beater.

The classic Greek dish Kota Avgolemono would have to be one
of the most nutritious, delicious and nourishing soups in the world.
Every child from a Greek household grows up with this soup
made with fresh chicken, rice and a tangy egg-lemon sauce.
It fills me with nostalgia for growing up at home with my parents,
but it also reminds me of how I, too, made the soup for my sons.
It soothes the soul on a cold day and makes for a substantial
meal by itself.

In a pot filled with water, combine the chicken with the celery,
onions, bay leaf, salt and peppercorns. Bring to a boil and
add the salt.

If you want, you can skim off any impurities until the stock is clear.
I don't bother to do this, as I strain the stock once the chicken
is cooked.

Once cooked, remove the chicken from the pot and strain your stock.

Return the stock back to the stove, bring to a boil,
check whether there is enough salt and then add the rice.
Boil until the rice is cooked.

To begin making the egg-lemon sauce, separate the
egg white from the yolks.

Beat the egg whites using the hand-held electric beater until soft
peaks form. Add the yolks and continue to beat.

Slowly pour in the lemon juice. Don't pour it all in at this stage.
Taste your sauce and, if it needs more lemon, add the rest.
Add the cornflour.

While continuing to beat the sauce, pour in three to four ladles'
worth of the chicken stock. Be careful to pour in a slow, steady
stream to prevent the egg mixture from curdling.

Transfer the egg-lemon sauce to the big pot and stir.

Shred the chicken and mix it into the soup. The soup should
be slightly tangy.

Frikasse Hirino Me Selino Avgolemono

Pork Casserole with Celery

1 small leg of free-range
or organic pork, deboned
and cut into cubes

2 full bunches of celery

2 potatoes, peeled and
cut into quarters

1 large onion,
finely diced

1 tsp cornflour

3 eggs, separated

1 cup of olive oil

juice of 2 lemons

2 cups of chicken stock

1 tsp celery salt

salt

pepper, freshly ground

You will also need
a hand-held electric
beater.

Crusty bread is a must
to mop up any sauce left
behind on the plate.

*This meal reminds me of winter at home with Mum and Dad.
Dad would sit at the table, and his job was to clean and
string the celery.*

*My family always use celery when making Frikasse, though some
people use lettuce leaves. Celery is the main vegetable and forms
the meal, as opposed to being in the background as flavouring.
Together with the pork, it is the hero. Once the dish is cooked,
we finish it off with an Avgolemono (egg-lemon) sauce.*

Wash the celery thoroughly and peel the strings off.
Cut the celery into ½ inch pieces.

In a large heavy pot, heat the olive oil and brown your pork
in batches. Once the meat has browned, add the onion,
celery, celery salt, pepper and stock.

Stir and taste the stock to ensure it has enough salt, and adjust
accordingly. Reduce your flame and gently simmer for about
30 minutes.

Add the potatoes and allow to cook for another 30 minutes.

At this stage you need to ensure that the meat has cooked
and the vegetables are tender.

Your pot should only contain about 1-2 cups of liquid.
If there is more, uncover and simmer to reduce the liquid.

To make the Avgolemono, place the egg whites in a large bowl.
Beat the egg whites with a pinch of salt using the hand-held
electric beater. Do so until soft peaks form.

Add the egg yolks then pour in the lemon juice in a slow,
steady stream. Don't stop beating. Add the cornflour.

Gradually beat in 3 ladles of the hot pork stock.

Return the sauce to the pot and gently swirl around to ensure
everything is mixed well.

CHRISTMAS

PSITO HIRINO STO FOURNO
SLOW-ROASTED PORK

SAFFRON PILAF

KALAMARIA YEMISTA
STUFFED CALAMARI

ORTIKIA LEMONATA PSITA STO FOURNO
ROASTED QUAILS WITH LEMON AND OREGANO

WATERMELON AND FETA SALAD

PASTITSIO

KEFTETHES
MEATBALLS

THE CHAOS OF THE
CHRISTMAS PREPARATIONS
ENDS AND I'M NOW READY
TO PREPARE THE TABLE
WITH MY BEST LINEN AND
FESTIVE EMBELLISHMENTS.
ALL THE FAMILY HEIRLOOMS
GRACE THE TABLE.

Psito Hirino Sto Fourno
Slow-roasted Pork

1 shoulder of free-range
or organic pork, well
scored by your butcher

3 onions

1 whole lemon,
skin and pith removed,
leaving just the flesh

zest of 1 orange

2 tbsp olive oil

1 cup of water

1 tsp fennel seeds

1 tsp celery salt

1 tsp cooking salt

pepper, freshly ground

Serve this amazing,
melt-in-your-mouth
pork dish with lemon
potatoes and salad.

*Slow-roasted Pork is a dish that we prepare for Christmas Day.
I wake up early and cook it in the oven very slowly for about
3-4 hours. It is truly worth the effort.*

*When preparing this dish, I like to use the Berkshire variety
of pork. However, any free-range or organic variety will do.
It is important to use the best-quality meat to get the best
end result.*

Preheat the oven to 200°C.

Pat the meat dry.

Toast the fennel seeds and gently grind them using a mortar
and pestle.

Slice the onions and arrange them on the bottom of the
baking dish. Slice the lemon and spread it over the onions.

Drizzle a little olive oil on the onions and sprinkle with salt.

Place your meat on top, and carefully but thoroughly rub the salt,
celery salt and pepper on it. It is important to season your
meat well.

Massage the meat thoroughly with olive oil. In a bow, combine the
salt, celery salt, pepper, orange zest and ground fennel seeds. Rub
this mixture into the meat, ensuring it goes into the scoring and
onto the underside. Add 1 cup of water to the baking dish.

Bake in the oven uncovered for about 30 minutes.

Take your pork out, reduce the temperature of the oven to 150°C,
cover the dish with foil and bake for a further 2 hours. Check the
meat after the first hour to make sure there is enough liquid
on the bottom, and add a little more if necessary.

After the final hour of cooking, take off the foil, increase the oven
temperature to approximately 200°C and continue to bake until
the meat browns and forms crackling.

Saffron Pilaf

2½ cups (450 g)
of basmati rice

3 tbsp (80 g) butter

6 tbsp oil

5 cups (1.2 L)
of vegetable
or chicken stock

10 threads of saffron,
ground with a little salt
in a mortar and pestle

1 tsp salt

1 tsp pepper

fresh parsley,
finely chopped
(to serve)

kefalotiri, grated
(to serve)

Saffron Pilaf is an excellent accompaniment to roast or braised meat or fish.

Melt the butter in a pan over high heat and combine it with the oil. When it begins to brown, add the rice and 1 teaspoon of salt, then toast, stirring constantly, until the rice turns opaque.

Pour in 5 cups of the stock along with the saffron and pepper. Bring to a boil.

Reduce the heat, cover, and simmer for about 20 minutes or until the rice has absorbed all the liquid and small holes appear on the surface.

Place a clean tea towel over the top of the pan, replace the lid, and remove from the heat.

Let the pilaf rest for 5-8 minutes. Serve sprinkled with finely chopped parsley and grated cheese.

Kalamaria Yemista
Stuffed Calamari

10 small to medium
calamari, with the
tentacles (ask your
fishmonger to clean them)

4 cups of baby spinach

1 long red chilli,
finely diced

½ cup of pine nuts

zest of 1 lemon

6 spring onions,
finely sliced

1 large onion,
finely diced

3 cloves of garlic,
finely crushed

1 tbsp medium-grain
rice for every calamari

1 cup of olive oil

1 cup of white wine

1 cup of water

a few sprigs of dill

1 tsp cooking salt

pepper, freshly ground

lemon wedges (to serve)

*Stuffed Calamari is a delicious dish that is easy to prepare.
It can be eaten at any time of the year for lunch or dinner.
For my family, though, we cook this the most during the
periods of Lent and Christmas.*

Clean the calamari under running cold water.
With kitchen scissors, cut the tentacles into small pieces.

Toast your pine nuts.

Measure your rice and wash thoroughly.

In a wide pan, sauté the onion, add the tentacles and cook until
light pink in colour. Add the chilli, spring onions, garlic and
lemon rind. Add the rice and toast it gently.

Stir the rice mixture and cook for a minute or so. Add the white
wine and let it evaporate, followed by a cup of water. Cook it
a little further, then turn off the flame.

Add the oil and spinach. The heat from the pan and the rice
will wilt the spinach.

Stir in the toasted pine nuts along with the dill, and season
with salt and pepper.

Take the 'tubes' of calamari and fill each three-quarters of the
way with the rice mixture. Using a toothpick, seal the ends.

Arrange the stuffed calamari in a non-stick tray, add a cup of water
and grill in the oven on a low setting for about 6–10 minutes — I
like to use the fan-forced grill mode. Be careful not to burn them.

Serve with lemon wedges.

Ortikia Lemonata Psita Sto Fourno

Roasted Quails with Lemon and Oregano

8-10 large quails

zest of 1 lemon

½ cup of olive oil

juice of 1 lemon

½ cup of water

1 tsp paprika

1 tsp dried oregano

salt

pepper

Wash your quails thoroughly.

Preheat the oven to 200°C.

Rub the birds all over with the olive oil (first inside then out), as well as the salt, pepper, oregano, paprika, lemon juice and lemon zest.

Arrange the birds side by side in an ovenproof dish and add the water. Cover the dish with aluminium foil and roast for 15 minutes.

Remove the foil and continue to bake for another 15-20 minutes, ensuring that the meat is cooked and the skin in golden.

Watermelon and Feta Salad

¼ – ½ watermelon
(depending on how
big or small it is),
cut into big cubes

½ red onion, thinly
sliced and soaked
in lemon juice for
about an hour

approx. 200 g
good-quality feta

olive oil

a few sprigs of mint

Soaking the onion
in lemon juice takes
away the acidity
and gives it
a sweet taste.
You can omit the
onion if you choose.

This salad reminds me of warm summer nights. Dad would be sitting in the backyard or possibly watering his vegetable garden, and Mum would bring out a bowl of watermelon slices, feta and crusty bread. Nothing else mattered, nothing more was needed; it was summer on a plate. The saltiness of the feta, together with the sweetness of the watermelon, somehow works.

Using a large platter, arrange the watermelon.

Cut the feta cheese into cubes and sprinkle over watermelon.

Remove the onion slices from the lemon juice and sprinkle them over the feta and watermelon.

Add the mint leaves.

Finish off the salad with a gentle drizzle of olive oil.
Serve with crusty bread.

Pastitsio

1 kg minced beef

1 can of tomatoes,
peeled and pureed

1 onion, grated

500 g thick
tube-shaped pasta
(such as macaroni
or penne)

2 cups (100 g)
kefalograviera or
other semi-hard cheese
(such as kefalotiri),
or one of each, grated

4 tbsp butter, melted,
plus extra for brushing

2 tbsp fine breadcrumbs

3 egg yolks,
lightly beaten

1 egg white,
lightly beaten

150 mL of olive oil

1 tablespoon
tomato paste

4 cups (1 L)
of béchamel sauce
(see recipe on page 234)

1 cup of water

a pinch of nutmeg, grated

a pinch of cinnamon,
ground (optional)

3 tbsp fresh parsley,
finely chopped

½ tsp sugar

salt

pepper

Pastitsio is a large dish consisting of pasta, minced meat and béchamel sauce cooked in a tapsi (Greek pan). It tastes even better when reheated and eaten the next day, and is served as a main meal with salad.

Heat half a cup (120 mL) of the oil in a large pan. Add the onion and cook over low heat, stirring occasionally, for 5 minutes until softened. Increase the heat to medium, add the minced beef, and cook for 10-15 minutes, stirring and breaking up the meat with the spoon until lightly browned.

Stir in the tomatoes, tomato paste, water, cinnamon (if desired), sugar and parsley, and season with salt and pepper. Reduce the heat and simmer for 15-20 minutes or until the liquid has reduced.

Remove from the heat and let cool for 5 minutes.

Fold in the egg white and half of the cheese. Taste and adjust the seasoning if necessary.

Fold the egg yolks and the remaining cheese into the béchamel sauce, season with salt and pepper, and stir in the nutmeg.

Bring a large pan of water to a boil and stir in salt and the remaining oil. Add the pasta and cook for 8-10 minutes or until al dente. Drain and toss with the melted butter, then let cool.

Preheat the oven to 180°C. Brush the ovenproof dish with melted butter and sprinkle with the breadcrumbs. Stir the cheese into the cooled pasta along with two cups of béchamel sauce. Mix well into the pasta.

Line the base of the prepared dish with half the pasta mixture and spread the meat mixture on top. Cover with the remaining pasta and pour the rest of the béchamel sauce over it.

Bake for about 1 hour or until the top is golden brown.

Let the dish stand for 15 minutes before cutting into serving pieces. Serve hot.

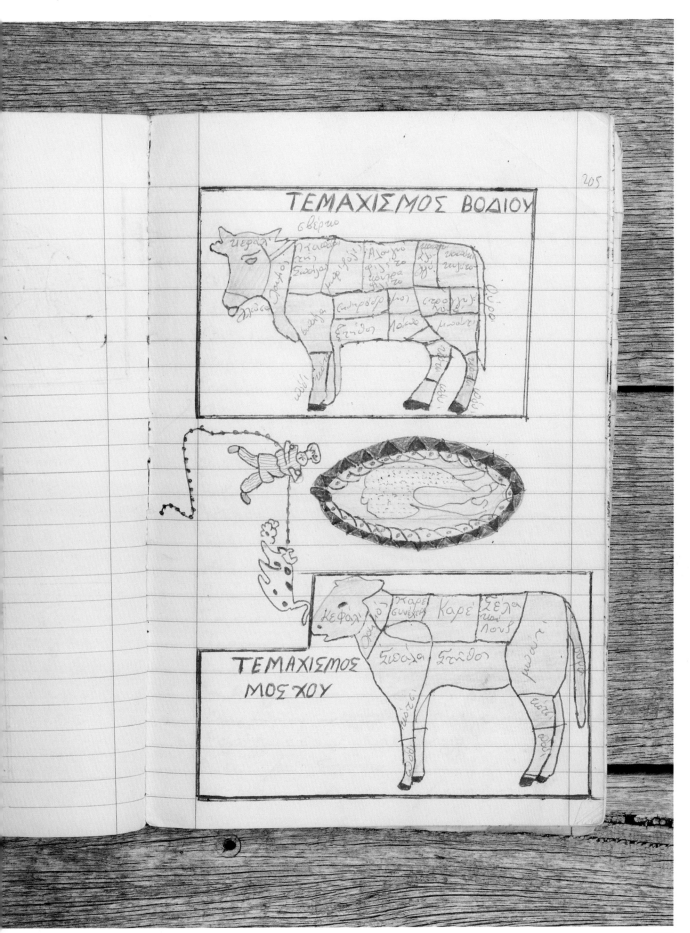

Keftethes

Meatballs

½ kg minced beef

½ kg minced pork

3 onions, finely grated

3 thick slices of stale bread, soaked in water and gently squeezed

2 eggs

2 tbsp olive oil

1 tsp dried oregano

½ bunch of parsley, finely chopped

4 tbsp fresh mint, finely shredded

1 tsp salt

pepper, freshly ground

sunflower oil (for frying)

flour (for dredging)

Using this meatball recipe and the Tomato Sauce recipe on page 235, you can create another meal. Once you have pan-fried your meatballs, add them to the tomato sauce and simmer for approximately 20 minutes to allow the flavours to merge. Serve with pilaf.

Keftethes remind me so much of my dad. He loved them, but to him they needed to be nice and soft rather than dry. Mum would not use as much bread as I would, so hers would be slightly drier. This would frustrate my dad and he would complain that Mum needed to use more onion and more bread. Whenever I would make them, he would say, 'Mmm, these meatballs smell of Kathy.' This is for you, Dad. You walk with me everywhere I go. I miss you.

Thoroughly combine the meats, onions, bread, eggs, olive oil, herbs, salt and pepper in a bowl. Refrigerate for an hour.

Check your mixture and, if you find it difficult to form balls, add a few more pieces of bread to absorb the extra moisture. Make the meatballs a little larger than walnut-sized balls and lay them out on a big tray.

Place some flour in a deep dish. Dust the meatballs lightly with flour, then pour in about half an inch of the sunflower oil into a wide, deep frypan and shallow-fry the meatballs.

Once you have fried them, serve the meatballs on a big platter with a delicious salad.

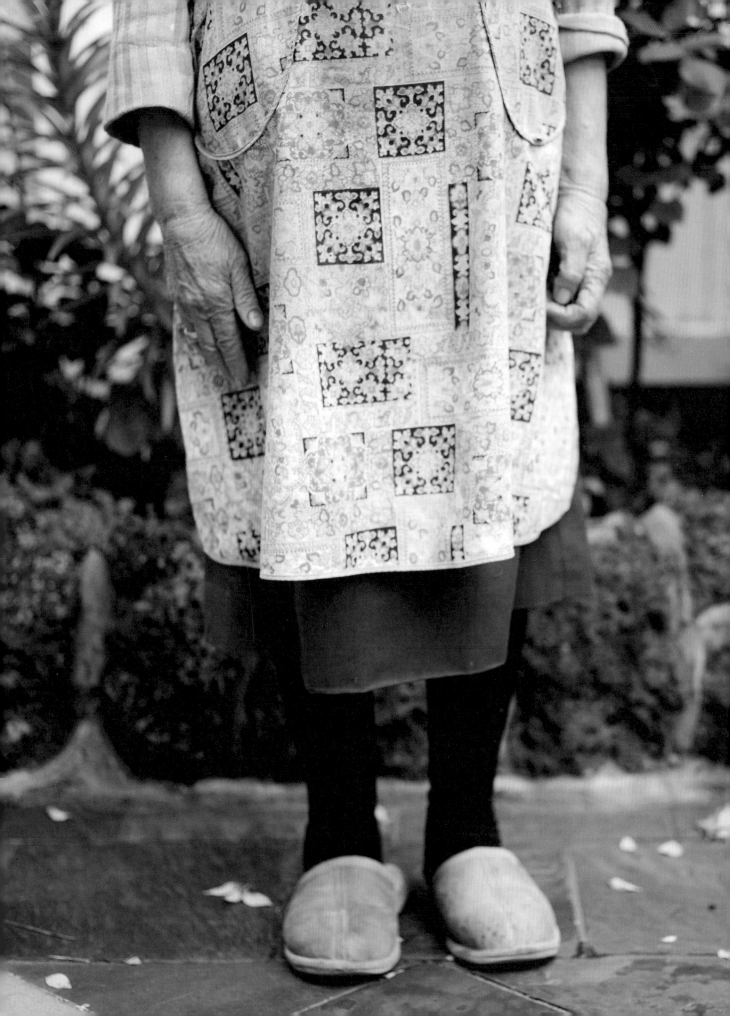

NEW YEAR

KOTOPITA
CHICKEN PIE

VASILOPITA
NEW YEAR'S CAKE

My family is still eating leftovers and relaxing after the Christmas feast. There are two exceptions: the chicken pie that is traditional from my mother's side of the family in Northern Greece, and the bread or cake tied to all of Greece.

I love New Year's Day. Mum and I would spend the week leading up to New Year's Eve cleaning, washing, ironing and cooking. It was very important that we didn't take the year's dirty linen into next year. No matter what was planned for New Year's Eve, we had to complete our chores first. Once we had completed our housework, Mum would start on the Vasilopita.

This is also the feast day of St Basil. On this day, all the women prepare Vasilopita, which can be either a cake or, as is tradition where I come from, a meat pie (Kreatopita or Kotopita). A coin is discreetly placed in the pie, and, as per an old Byzantine custom, we slice the Vasilopita. The person who finds the coin hidden in his or her slice gets good luck for the year.

On New Year's Day, we would decorate the table and my father would sit in the middle. It was his job to turn the pie three times: once for the Virgin Mary, once for Christ and once for the house. Following this, he slices a piece for everyone in the family, starting with the eldest. We would all then stab our piece to find the coin before devouring the amazing pie that Mum had made.

Kotopita

Chicken Pie

5 chicken Marylands

6 spring onions, finely sliced

3 onions, finely diced

dough (see 'Basic Dough' recipe on page 234)

½ cup of coarse semolina

½ cup butter, melted

1 cup of cream

1 cup of kefalotiri, finely grated

5 eggs, beaten

½ cup of olive oil

a pinch of allspice

sugar

1 tsp salt

½ tsp white pepper

You will also need a 40 cm round baking dish.

Instead of a sweet cake or bread, Mum would traditionally make Chicken Pie for New Year's Day.

Wash your chicken and poach it in a big pot gently until it falls off the bone. Discard bones and chop chicken meat into pieces.

In a pan, sauté the onions with the salt then add the chicken pieces and the spring onions.

Take off the heat and allow to cool.

Once cooled, add the eggs, cheese, pepper, cream and semolina. Taste the salt level and adjust accordingly. Add the pinch of allspice.

For this pie we will make a different pastry. Make dough using the 'Basic Dough' recipe (page 234), then divide it into ten balls. Allow to rest. Roll out five balls into the size of a plate.

Combine the olive oil and melted butter, then brush each of the five dough pieces with this mixture.

Lay them one on top of the other on a plate, cover with cling wrap and refrigerate. Repeat with the remaining five dough pieces.

Thoroughly brush the baking dish with the butter and oil mixture.

Take the first set of dough out of the fridge and roll each piece out so that they are about 1 inch bigger than your baking dish.

Arrange the chicken mixture on top of the pastry.

Take the second stack of pastry and roll it to the size of the baking dish, as one sheet. Place it on top and fold in the bottom sheet to seal the chicken and form a crust. Gently roll and pinch the seal closed.

Brush the top pastry with the oil and butter, and bake at 180°C for about 1 hour. At the halfway mark, check to make sure the pie has not burnt. Cover with foil if the pastry is browning too quickly.

Once out of the oven, sprinkle with a little sugar to ensure it is sweet. The combination of chicken, pastry and sugar is divine.

Vasilopita

New Year's Cake

4 cups of self-raising
flour, sifted

1 tsp bicarbonate of soda

1 tsp vanilla extract or
paste

3 eggs

1 cup of sunflower
or grapeseed oil

1 cup of warm milk

1 cup of orange juice,
freshly squeezed

1 tsp each of ginger,
cinnamon and nutmeg

2 cups of caster sugar

You will also need
an electric mixer.

*I was given this recipe by my neighbour Dimi. Her husband,
Milton, and I have been neighbours since I was 17 years old.
He arrived in Australia at 19 years of age from the island
of Mytilini and at first lived with his sister Alexandra.*

*The recipe was originally devised by Milton's mother, Anna,
who has sadly passed away. But through this recipe, her legacy
lives on. It is a beautiful cake and, while it is called Vasilopita
(meaning 'New Year's Cake'), it can be made at any time
of the year — with the exception that you don't insert a coin
in the cake.*

Preheat the oven to 150°C.

Beat the oil and the sugar using the paddle-wheel attachment
of an electric mixer. Add the eggs and beat until the mixture
is creamy and fluffy.

Quickly stir the bicarbonate of soda into the cup of orange juice;
it will bubble away. Pour it into the mixture and continue
to beat at a low speed.

Add the spices while still beating, then add the warm milk.
When combined, stop beating and fold in the flour.

Take a one-dollar coin and wrap it in foil.

Butter a large (40-centimetre) baking dish or two small cake pans.

Pour the cake mixture into the baking dish. Insert the coin
in a spot close to the edge.

Bake for an hour.

SWEETS

YIAOURTOPITA
YOGHURT CAKE WITH LEMON

RIZOGALO
CREAMY RICE PUDDING

PASTELI
SESAME SEED SLAB

AMIGTHALOTA

PAXIMATHIA
BISCOTTI

YOGHURT WITH HONEY AND WALNUT

KOULOURAKIA

TSOUREKI

MELOMAKARONA
HONEY WALNUT BISCUITS

BAKLAVA

LOUKOUMADES
HONEY DOUGHNUTS

KARITHOPITA
WALNUT CAKE

AMIGTHALOTA AHLATHIA
MARZIPAN PEARS

GALAKTOBOUREKO

KOURABIETHES
GREEK SHORTBREAD BISCUITS

GALATOPITA
CUSTARD PIE

REVANI
MOIST SEMOLINA CAKE

HALVA

VISSINO GLYKO
SOUR CHERRIES

GLYKA TOU KOUTALIOU
FIG SPOON SWEET

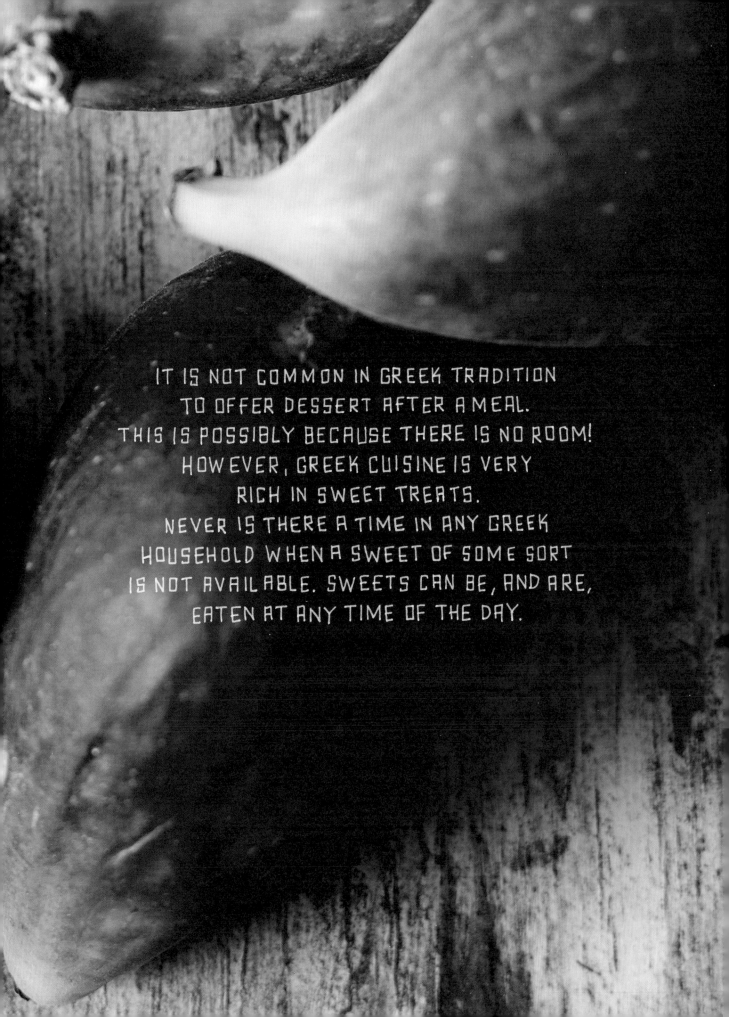

IT IS NOT COMMON IN GREEK TRADITION
TO OFFER DESSERT AFTER A MEAL.
THIS IS POSSIBLY BECAUSE THERE IS NO ROOM!
HOWEVER, GREEK CUISINE IS VERY
RICH IN SWEET TREATS.
NEVER IS THERE A TIME IN ANY GREEK
HOUSEHOLD WHEN A SWEET OF SOME SORT
IS NOT AVAILABLE. SWEETS CAN BE, AND ARE,
EATEN AT ANY TIME OF THE DAY.

Yiaourtopita

Yoghurt Cake with Lemon

2 tsp lemon zest

3 cups of
self-raising flour

3 tsp baking powder

250 g butter, softened at
room temperature

1½ cups of yoghurt
(preferably full-cream)

6 eggs

icing sugar (for dusting)

1½ cups of sugar

a pinch of salt

You will also need
an electric mixer.

You don't need an excuse or reason to make Yiaourtopita, which is a delicious cake for any occasion. Make it for your family and friends, and serve it with a cup of coffee or tea.

Preheat the oven to 180°C.

Grease and flour a cake tin (approx. 26 centimetres in diameter).

Separate the eggs by placing the whites in a clean stainless-steel bowl. Whisk these with a pinch of salt until soft peaks form.

In a separate bowl, beat the butter combined with the sugar using the paddle-wheel attachment of the electric mixer.

Add the egg yolks one at a time, followed by the lemon zest then the yoghurt.

Using a big spoon and with the mixer on the slowest speed setting, gradually add the flour and baking powder.

Fold in the egg whites.

Bake the cake for 40–45 minutes. Confirm that the cake is fully cooked by inserting a knife in the middle – you'll know it's ready when the knife comes out clean.

Once out of the oven and while still hot, dust the cake with icing sugar.

Rizogalo
Creamy Rice Pudding

1 cup of
medium-grain rice

2 L full-cream milk, warm

1½ L water

2 tsp vanilla paste,
or the seeds of 1 pod
of vanilla

2½ cups of sugar

1 level tsp salt

Dutch cinnamon
(as garnish)

Everybody loves Rizogalo; it is comfort food at its finest. I always make a big batch and share it with my neighbours and friends. Any leftovers go into the fridge, to be enjoyed the next day. Making Rizogalo is so satisfying, as I have to stir the pot gently and continuously and wait for the rice and milk to thicken. I am always overcome by a feeling that I am nurturing my family.

In a large saucepan, bring the water to a boil. Add the salt followed by the rice, and stir until the rice absorbs all the liquid.

Gradually add the warm milk. Keep stirring patiently until the mixture thickens — this does take a while.

When the mixture has thickened, add the sugar and vanilla paste or seeds.

Simmer for a further 10 minutes.

Pour into individual bowls. Sprinkle with cinnamon and enjoy.

Pasteli

Sesame Seed Slab

½ kg sesame seeds,
toasted in the oven

½ kg walnuts

½ kg honey

1 cup of flaked almonds

½ 25 g packet
of vanilla sugar

1½ tbsp sugar

Pasteli is easy to make and keeps for long periods. Growing up, whenever someone would arrive back from Greece, the one thing we would anxiously await to receive was the Pasteli.

It is one of the most ancient of Greek food items, and will continue to be enjoyed by many.

This recipe makes a beautiful Pasteli that looks amazing as well as being delicious.

Firstly, toast your sesame seeds in the oven.

Combine the honey with the sugar and vanilla sugar in a saucepan, and heat over a medium flame until it starts to bubble.

Add the sesame seeds. Cook slowly, stirring constantly for about 10-15 minutes until the mixture develops a gold colouring.

Mix in the walnuts.

Spread some baking paper in a shallow tray or stone cutting board. Pour the hot sesame mixture onto it and work the surface with a spatula until it has a uniform thickness of about ½ inch.

Take some baking paper, place it on top of the sesame mixture, and use a rolling pin to gently even out the surface.

Remove the baking paper, sprinkle the flaked almonds on top and press in.

Cut into diamond shapes and enjoy.

Amigthalota

3 cups of almond meal

2 tbsp apricot jam

zest of 1 lemon

1 cup of caster sugar

3 egg whites

a pinch of salt

flaked almonds
(as garnish)

Amigthalo means 'almond' in Greek. It may look difficult to pronounce, but I assure you these delectable almond meal biscuits will become a favourite. At the Sweet Greek stall, Amigthalota are one of our bestsellers and are the dessert of choice for those looking for a gluten-free treat.

Preheat the oven to 150°C.

Line a baking tray with baking paper.

Gently whisk the egg whites and the salt until soft peaks form.

Combine the egg whites with the almond meal, caster sugar, apricot jam and lemon zest.

Transfer teaspoon-sized batches of the mixture onto the baking paper, and then sprinkle with flaked almonds. Alternatively, you can use a piping bag and create little logs, which can then be sprinkled with flaked almonds.

Bake for 10–15 minutes.

Once baked, spread apricot jam on one biscuit or log and sandwich it with another.

Paximathia

Biscotti

1 cup of almonds, toasted

2 kg self-raising flour

3 cups of sunflower oil

1 Greek coffee cup
of ouzo

2 cups of orange juice

2 cups of water

2 tsp vanilla extract

1 packet of aniseed

½ packet of cloves

3 sticks of cinnamon

1 tsp Dutch cinnamon

2 cups of sugar

1 tsp salt

Paximathia are very similar to biscotti. Traditionally we serve them, along with a cup of coffee, to visitors when we have lost someone dear to us. However, these biscuits are also available all year round.

There are countless recipes and variations. Many years ago, in my quest to find the perfect Paximathia recipe, I discovered that my cousin Kathy's recipe was the best. Kathy, the daughter of my dad's brother Paul, is an excellent cook, and she was kind enough to share this recipe with me. I now share it with you. Don't be overwhelmed by the ingredients — it is worth the effort spending an afternoon making Paximathia.

Preheat the oven to 180°C.

Boil the water with the aniseed, cloves and cinnamon sticks for approximately 20 minutes.

In a large bowl, mix together the oil, sugar, vanilla and salt.

Add the orange juice and ouzo.

Strain the water and add it to the mixture followed by the Dutch cinnamon.

Add the flour and almonds, and work the mixture into a pliable dough.

Take the dough and roll it into the shape of a log.
Bake it for 20-30 minutes.

Take the log out of the oven and use a serrated knife to slice the log into biscuits diagonally across. Bake again for another 20-30 minutes, making sure that both sides of the Paximathia are golden.

Cool on a rack, store in an airtight container.

Yoghurt with Honey and Walnut

200 g of good-quality
Greek yoghurt (at the
Sweet Greek shop we
have yoghurt by Dodonis)

2-3 tbsp Attiki honey

a handful of walnuts,
lightly toasted and
with skins rubbed
gently using a towel

a pinch of Dutch cinnamon

*As simple as this recipe is, its success lies in using the best
ingredients. A favourite in all Greek families, Yoghurt with Honey
and Walnut can be eaten at any time of the day — it is a great
breakfast alternative, can be eaten as a light dinner, or even
as a light dessert.*

Spoon the yoghurt into a beautiful bowl.

Drizzle the honey over it.

Sprinkle the walnuts and the cinnamon.

Sit back and enjoy.

Koulourakia

zest of 1 orange

zest of 1 lemon

1 tsp baking powder

7-9 cups of self-raising flour, sifted

250 g good-quality unsalted butter

6 eggs (1 for glazing)

1 cup of milk

1 cup of orange juice

25 g packet of vanilla sugar

2 cups of caster sugar

1 tbsp milk (for glazing)

sesame seeds (as garnish — optional)

During Holy Week, all the women are busy baking and preparing everything to celebrate on Easter Sunday. Koulourakia are made in the days leading up to midnight mass on Easter Saturday.

Preheat the oven to 180°C.

Cream the butter and caster sugar until light and fluffy. Add five eggs, one at a time.

Add the milk, orange juice, orange zest, lemon zest and vanilla sugar. The mixture may curdle at this stage, but don't worry because adding the flour will rectify this.

Sift the baking powder with 2 cups of the flour and add to the mixture. Keep adding flour, one cup at a time to form a soft, pliable dough. Let it rest while you tidy up.

Shape pieces of dough into little logs and then twist them. You can also plait them.

Beat the remaining egg with 1 tablespoon of milk and use to glaze the logs. Sprinkle with sesame seeds.

Bake for about 20 minutes then allow to cool.

Tsoureki

zest of 1 orange

zest of 1 lemon

2 kg strong white baker's flour (we call this 'special white')

2 tsp bread improver

200 g fresh yeast

1 sachet of dried yeast

250 g butter

10 eggs, plus 1 more for glazing

1 cup of milk

2 tbsp olive oil

1 tsp masticha, ground (achieved by grinding in a mortar and pestle with a little sugar)

2 packets of mahlepi

25 g packet of vanilla sugar

2¼ cups of sugar

1 tsp salt

sesame seeds and flaked almonds (as garnish)

At Easter time we insert a red dyed egg in the Tsoureki.

Tsoureki is an aromatic sweetbread that represents Easter. Together with all the other Easter goodies we bake, Tsoureki breaks the Lenten fast. It is traditionally made with a red egg in the centre.

The recipes are varied, but common to all is the use of masticha and mahlepi. The particular aroma comes from the seeds of the Mediterranean wild cherry and gives Tsoureki its distinct flavours. These days, it is not uncommon to use four key spices: mahlepi, masticha, vanilla and cardamon.

Preheat the oven to 180°C.

Dissolve both the fresh and dried yeast into a teacup of lukewarm water, and mix well with half a cup of flour. Leave this mixture for 15 minutes and allow to rise.

Combine the sugar, oil, masticha and mahlepi, then add the vanilla sugar.

Once the yeast mixture is ready, combine the two mixtures together. Add the rinds of both the orange and the lemon. Then add the milk.

Using your hands, stir constantly and add one egg at a time. Add the flour and bread improver, and knead.

Melt your butter into a bowl. Dip your hands into the butter and continue to gently knead the dough, stretch and fold in. Do this until all the butter has been incorporated.

Cover the bowl with cling wrap, a towel and a blanket, and place in a warm spot to allow the dough to rise. This will take approximately 2 hours.

Punch down and, with well-floured hands, separate the dough into batches.

Make three long ropes and braid. Continue to do this until all the mixture is used up.

Line a baking tray with baking paper and place the braids on it. Place in a warm spot again and allow to rise.

Using the extra egg, glaze the Tsoureki by brushing it with egg wash. Afterwards, sprinkle with sesame seeds and flaked almonds.

Bake for 20–25 minutes.

Melomakarona
Honey Walnut Biscuits

Biscuit

6-9 cups of plain flour
(you need to form a soft
dough that doesn't stick
to your hands)

2 tsp baking powder

zest of 1 orange

2 cups of grapeseed oil

juice of 1 orange

½ cup beer

1 tsp cinnamon

½ tsp nutmeg, ground

½ tsp cloves, ground

1½ cups of caster sugar

Syrup

2 cups of honey

4 cups of water

1½ cups of sugar

1 cup of walnuts,
finely crushed
(for sprinkling on top)

Melomakarona are a traditional sweet, baked at Easter and Christmas time. However, they can be baked all year round and enjoyed with a cup of coffee. No feast is complete without them. As they are dairy-free they can be enjoyed during any period when we are fasting.

Preheat the oven to 180°C.

In a big bowl, combine the oil, caster sugar, juice, zest and beer. I prefer to use my hands, as the warmth of my hands dissolves the sugar.

Sift the flour and combine it with the baking powder and spices. Add these to the wet mixture, cup by cup, until you have a soft, pliable dough. If your dough is too soft, add more flour. It should not stick to your hands.

Take small pieces about the size of a walnut (or slightly bigger, if you prefer) and shape these into rounded logs about 7 centimetres long.

Using a fork, press down on the logs to form a pattern. Bake your biscuits for about 25 minutes.

While the biscuits are baking, create the syrup by simmering the honey, sugar and water for 5 minutes. Remove any scum that appears on the surface.

Cool the biscuits after they have finished baking. Dip each one into the hot syrup for a few seconds and then sprinkle with crushed walnuts. Break one Melomakarona open to ensure that the syrup has been absorbed.

Baklava

Pastry

1 packet (approx. 375 g)
of filo pastry

4 cups of walnuts,
chopped

250 g unsalted butter

2 tsp cinnamon

½ tsp cloves, ground

½ cup of caster sugar

cloves (as garnish)

Syrup

1 wedge of lemon

a squeeze of lemon juice

1 cup of honey

2 cups of water

3 cups of sugar

Everybody knows about Baklava. There are so many variations of it depending on where it comes from and who it is made by. Our Baklava is a traditional one using filo pastry and walnuts. I'm sure you will enjoy it.

Preheat the oven to 180°C.

Combine the walnuts, caster sugar, cinnamon and ground cloves in a bowl.

Melt the butter. Start with four pastry sheets and brush butter on each one, to line a rectangular baking tray (use the size of the filo sheet as your guide).

Spread some of the walnut mixture on the sheets.

Add another four layers of pastry, buttering each one, then spread the walnuts again. Keep doing this until all the ingredients have finished. It's good to finish with about six layers of filo pastry on top.

Using a sharp knife, score the baklava into diamonds, then pour any remaining butter over the top. Insert a clove into each diamond and bake for about 45 minutes.

Create the syrup by boiling the water, sugar, honey, lemon juice and the wedge of lemon for about 10 minutes. Let cool.

Once the Baklava is out of the oven and while still hot, pour the cooled syrup over the top.

Loukoumades

Honey Doughnuts

2 cups of plain flour,
sifted twice

2 sachets of dried yeast

250 mL warm water

1 tsp sugar

½ tsp salt

oil (for deep-frying)

honey, walnuts
and cinnamon
(to serve)

Combine the yeast with a little warm water. Add ½ a cup of the flour and allow to sit until frothy.

In a bowl, sift your flour. Add the yeast slurry, followed by the sugar, salt and water, and mix until you have a wonderful elastic dough with a batter-like consistency.

Allow to rest, covered and in a warm spot for about an hour. Heat the oil and start making little balls with a spoon.

Deep-fry the balls. Drizzle with honey and sprinkle with walnuts and cinnamon.

Karithopita
Walnut Cake

Cake

3 cups of walnuts,
gently roasted and
coarsely ground

12 eggs

2 cups of breadcrumbs

1 tsp baking powder

1 tbsp cocoa powder

2 tbsp cognac or brandy

1 level tsp cinnamon

1½ cups of caster sugar

Syrup

2 cups of water

1 stick of cinnamon

2½ cups of sugar

Karithopita was the first cake I made from Mum's new cookbook by Sofia Skoura. It was my mum's new Tselemende and we were all so excited. It was liberating to know that we now had all these new recipes to make. I became well-known among our family and friends as the best Karithopita maker.

The recipe that follows is based on Sofia Skoura's with the exception that I add 12 eggs as opposed to eight. Furthermore, to give the Karithopita a beautiful chocolate colour, I add a tablespoon of cocoa.

Preheat the oven to 180°C.

Toast and roughly chop your walnuts, then combine them with the cinnamon and cocoa.

Separate the egg yolks from the whites. Beat the yolks with the caster sugar until light and fluffy. Add the cognac or brandy followed by the walnut mixture.

Beat the egg whites to form soft peaks. Gently fold into the mixture, alternating the egg whites with the breadcrumbs. Continue to do this until all ingredients have been incorporated.

Place in a greased rectangular tin and bake for about 40–45 minutes.

Create the syrup by bringing the sugar, water and cinnamon stick to a boil and then simmering for 5–10 minutes.

Pour the hot syrup over the hot cake and allow to sit with a towel over the top for about an hour.

Cut into diamonds and serve.

Amigthalota Ahlathia
Marzipan Pears

1 kg almonds, blanched,
dried and ground

3 tbsp fine semolina

3 egg whites

3 tbsp honey

1 cup of rosewater

2 cups of caster sugar

25 g packet
of vanilla sugar

2 cups of pure
icing sugar

cloves (as garnish)

It's a good idea
to re-coat your little
'pears' after a couple
of hours to make them
completely white.

These beautiful delicacies are traditionally made on Greek islands such as Hydra and Mytilini. They are a celebratory treat offered at weddings and christenings. At christenings, we pin a pink or blue bow with a clove to the pears.

I always make a platter of Amigthalota Ahlathia for Christmas. Once again, I learnt to make these from my neighbours Milton and Dimi, as he is from Mytilini. Milton's sister Alexandra also makes them.

Start this recipe a day ahead.

Dry the blanched almonds in the oven, then grind them finely in a food processor.

Combine the egg whites (lightly beaten with a fork), almonds, semolina, caster and vanilla sugars, and half the rosewater in a bowl, and mix to make a pliable paste. Allow this mixture to rest overnight, covered and in the fridge.

The next day, knead the paste again while adding in the honey. If the paste is too dry, add a little more rosewater. If it is too wet and can't be moulded, add a little more semolina.

Preheat your oven to 180°C.

Mould small amounts of the paste into pear-like shapes and insert a clove on top. Bake for 15–20 minutes.

Once out of the oven, brush with rosewater and thoroughly dredge with icing sugar.

Galaktoboureko

Pastry

1 packet (375 g)
of filo pastry

1½ cups of fine semolina

1 cup of cornflour

1 vanilla bean, split and
seeds scraped

250 g unsalted butter,
melted, plus extra
for greasing

5 eggs, lightly beaten

3 L milk

2 cups of caster sugar

25 g packet
of vanilla sugar

1 tsp salt

Syrup

½ tsp lemon juice

2 cups of water

1 stick of cinnamon

2½ cups of sugar

Galaktoboureko is a delicious semolina custard with filo on the bottom and top, and with a light syrup poured over. It can be seen as the Greek version of a vanilla slice. At the Sweet Greek stall, it is our signature sweet, selling up to five trays every Saturday.

Preheat the oven to 180°C.

Set aside ½ litre of milk and pour the rest into a saucepan. Heat it gently, adding the salt, vanilla sugar, vanilla seeds and pod.

Pour in the semolina and, using a whisk, keep beating to avoid the semolina going lumpy. Keep cooking it for about 15 minutes.

Combine the remaining milk with the cornflour to make a paste, and quickly pour it into the semolina mixture while continuing to beat constantly. Add the caster sugar and cook for a further 5 minutes. This will create a custard, and to make it successfully you must constantly beat and stir the mixture to prevent it from sticking and becoming lumpy. The effort is worth it.

Add the lightly beaten eggs. Do not stop stirring at this point — you need to ensure that the eggs don't cook and the custard doesn't curdle.

Grease your baking dish. You will need a long, deep dish for this amount of custard.

Melt the butter. Divide your filo pastry in half and start layering while buttering each layer. Make sure to hang some pastry over the tray so as you can wrap up the custard.

Spread the custard over the base then completely cover with remaining pastry sheets, buttering each layer. Trim the top pastry's edges and gently cut the filo into squares without going through to the custard.

Bake for about 50 minutes.

Create the syrup by boiling the sugar, water, cinnamon stick and lemon juice for 5 minutes.

Cool the syrup, remove cinnamon stick and pour it over the hot Galaktoboureko.

Kourabiethes
Greek Shortbread Biscuits

2 cups of plain flour,
sifted

1 cup of cornflour

1 cup of almonds,
toasted and roughly
chopped

250 g good-quality
unsalted butter

2 egg yolks

2 tbsp ouzo

1 tsp vanilla extract

½ tsp cinnamon

cloves

½ cup of caster sugar

pure icing sugar

rosewater

Kourabiethes are shortbread biscuits dusted with icing sugar. They are a treat on any occasion. Display them on a platter and use rose petals to accentuate the soft white mounds of icing sugar.

Preheat the oven to 180°C.

Cream the butter and sugar until light and fluffy. Add the yolks and vanilla. Slowly add both flours and the almonds, then the ouzo and cinnamon. Make sure the dough is soft and pliable.

Roll the dough into little walnut-shaped balls and, using your thumb, make a dent. Insert a clove in the dent.

Bake for 15-20 minutes on a baking tray lined with baking paper. Afterwards, while still hot, brush with rosewater. Sift icing sugar into a large bowl. Toss the Kourabiethes in this. Allow to cool.

Galatopita
Custard Pie

approx. 5 sheets
of filo pastry

200 g fine semolina

3 eggs

butter (for brushing
the pastry)

2 L milk

2 tsp vanilla extract

2 cups of sugar

1 tsp salt

icing sugar (for dusting)

cinnamon (for dusting)

Galatopita is a creamy semolina custard that is baked with filo pastry on the bottom and as a crust. There are many variations of this recipe, depending on which region of Greece you are from, but below is my mum's recipe. I grew up on this delicious pie, as did my boys. Often, Mum would bake during the day so that my boys could have a huge piece after school. It is very similar to Galaktoboureko except it doesn't have the syrup and usually has thinner layers.

In a large saucepan, warm your milk. Do not let it boil.

Sprinkle in the semolina and salt, and whisk continuously to ensure that no lumps form.

Continue stirring for about 30 minutes to form a delicious, thick custard.

Once the custard has cooked, take the saucepan off the heat.

Add your sugar, vanilla extract and the lightly beaten eggs. Do not stop stirring at this point — you need to ensure that the eggs don't cook and the custard doesn't curdle.

Allow your custard to rest and turn your oven to 180°C.

Prepare the filo pastry in your baking dish by layering and brushing butter on each layer.

Pour the custard in and bake for approximately 40-45 minutes.

Once out of the oven, cool and dust with icing sugar and cinnamon.

Revani

Moist Semolina Cake

Cake

1 cup of semolina

1 cup of almonds,
blanched, toasted
and roughly chopped

2 cups of self-raising
flour, sifted

2 tsp baking powder

zest of 1 lemon

6 eggs

250 g butter,
at room temperature

juice of 2 oranges

2 tbsp cognac or brandy

1 cup of caster sugar

shredded coconut
(as garnish)

Syrup

1 wedge of lemon

3½ cups of water

3 cups of sugar

You will also need
an electric mixer.

Revani is a moist semolina cake that has become a family favourite. Over the years it has taken pride of place at many celebrations. I would often say that the true test of a good cake is when friends and family ask for the recipe.

At the Sweet Greek shop, we make Revani almost daily. It is a favourite with many customers.

Preheat your oven to 175°C.

Make the syrup by bringing the sugar, water and lemon wedge to a boil, then simmering for 10 minutes. Take the syrup off the heat and cool down completely.

To begin making the cake, cream the butter with the sugar using the paddle-wheel attachment of the electric mixer. Add the eggs one at a time, then the lemon zest. Reduce the mixer's speed and add the orange juice and cognac.

Combine the semolina and the baking powder. Slowly add the self-raising flour to the mixing bowl, followed by the combined semolina and baking powder.

Mix in the almonds.

Thoroughly butter and flour a square cake tin, then pour in the mixture.

Bake for approximately 45 minutes.

Once the cake is ready, take it out of the oven and pour the cold syrup over the hot cake. Cover with a tea towel for about an hour, allowing the cake to soak up the syrup.

Cut into squares and garnish by sprinkling shredded coconut on top.

Halva

<u>Cake</u>

1 cup of walnuts,
roughly chopped

2 cups of coarse semolina

1 tbsp butter

½ cup of grapeseed oil

<u>Syrup</u>

1 stick of cinnamon

10 cloves

4 cups of water

3 cups of sugar

In a medium saucepan, create a syrup by bringing the water, sugar, cinnamon stick and cloves to a boil. Allow to simmer for 10 minutes to bring all the flavours together.

In another pan, heat up the oil and the butter. Once the butter has melted and stops bubbling, add the semolina and walnuts and continue to stir until the semolina takes on a light golden colour. This does take a while, but be careful not to burn it.

Remove the pan from the stove. Pour in the syrup and keep stirring. You need to be very careful because the mixture will bubble and sputter. Once all the syrup has been absorbed, put the pan back onto the flame and cook until the Halva easily comes off the sides of the pan.

You can pack the mixture into a Tupperware mould, or lay it out in a baking tray and cut it into diamonds. Enjoy the Halva with a nice cup of coffee.

Vissino Glyko
Sour Cherries

1 kg sour cherries*

2 cups of water

juice of 1 lemon

1 vanilla bean, split and
seeds scraped

½ cup of glucose

1 kg sugar

These cherries can be
served with a cold glass
of water. You can also
add them to your yoghurt
as a dessert or even
over vanilla ice-cream.
They really are worth it!

*Sour cherries
 are available
 in mid-December.

Start this recipe a day ahead.

Thoroughly wash the cherries and remove the pips.

In a medium pan, create the syrup by boiling the water,
sugar and cherries for 10 minutes. Let stand for 24 hours.

The next day, bring to a boil again and simmer until the syrup thickens.

Add the vanilla, lemon juice and glucose, and cook for
another 5 minutes.

Let cool and then pack into sterilised jars.

Glyka Tou Koutaliou

Fig Spoon Sweet

1 kg green unripe figs

juice of 1 lemon

2 cups of water,
plus additional
water for boiling

1 vanilla bean,
seeds scraped

10 cloves

½ cup of glucose

800 g sugar

Start this recipe two days ahead.

Wash the figs thoroughly. Put them in a pot of water and bring to a boil for 5 minutes. Throw this water out and repeat the process for another 5 minutes with fresh water.

Drain the figs overnight.

The next day, make the syrup by boiling the 2 cups of water along with the sugar, cloves and vanilla for 5–10 minutes.

Add the figs and let stand for 24 hours.

The following day, bring the syrup with the figs to the boil and then lower the flame. Simmer until the syrup thickens. At this stage, add the lemon juice and the glucose.

Allow the figs to cool in the syrup, and then arrange in glass jars that have been sterilised. The figs should be submerged.

BASICS

BASIC DOUGH

BÉCHAMEL SAUCE

CHICKEN STOCK

FISH STOCK

TOMATO SAUCE

Basic Dough

---

1 kg special plain
white flour (it is
important to use this;
however, an alternative
would be '00' pizza
flour)

½ cup of olive oil

2 tbsp white vinegar

approx. 2-2½ cups
of warm water

1 tsp salt

*This is a simple dough
recipe that is perfect
for any pie dish such
a Spanakopita or
chicken pie.*

Using a stainless-steel bowl,
pour in your flour and
mix in the salt.

Make a well in the middle
and pour in the vinegar,
oil and a bit of the water.

Using your hands, swirl the
mixture and keep adding
water until you have a
beautiful, soft, pliable dough.

Allow your dough to rest for
at least 1 hour. Cover well with
cling wrap.

Béchamel Sauce

---

100 g plain flour

100 g butter

3 eggs

1 L milk

1 bay leaf

a pinch of nutmeg

½ tsp salt

½ tsp white pepper

Warm your milk in a saucepan
with the bay leaf. Set aside.

In a pot, melt the butter,
add the flour and stir vigorously.
Continue stirring for approx.
3-5 minutes in order to take
away the flour taste.

Take the pot off the stove
and gently whisk in the milk.
Continue whisking to ensure
no lumps are formed.
Return to the stove and cook
for another 5 minutes or so.

Season with salt, pepper and
nutmeg. Beat the eggs and
add them to the cooked sauce.

Chicken Stock

---

1 bag of chicken carcases

1 bag of chicken necks

6 chicken wings

2 sticks of celery

2 onions

4 L water

1 bay leaf

2 tsp salt

10 peppercorns

*Use this recipe whenever
you require chicken stock.
When this stock is used
for Pilaf, it makes the Pilaf
taste amazing. This stock can
also be frozen for future use.*

In a large stock pot, combine
all your ingredients and fill
the pot with cold water.

Place on the stove and bring
to a boil, then allow to simmer
gently for 2-3 hours.

Remove from the heat
and strain.

Fish Stock

Tomato Sauce

---

1 bag of fish heads
and bones

2 sticks of celery

1 carrot

2 onions

½ cup of olive oil

4 L water

1 bay leaf

1 tsp salt

10 peppercorns

*Like the chicken stock,
this fish stock can be
frozen for future use.*

*Ask your fishmonger for
various bones and heads
from fish that have been
filleted. Avoid salmon bones.*

Combine all the ingredients
in a stock pot with water and
bring to a boil. Turn down the
heat and simmer gently
for 2–3 hours.

Strain and use as required.

---

3 cans of tomatoes,
crushed

1 piece of reggiano rind
(which can be obtained
from your local deli)

½ cup olive oil

1 tbsp tomato paste

a pinch of chilli flakes

1 tsp sweet paprika

6–10 basil leaves

1 tsp sugar

1 tbsp salt

pepper

*I like to have this sauce on
reserve for whenever I need to
make a tomato-based recipe.*

Combine all the ingredients
into a heavy saucepan.
Stir and bring to a boil.

Reduce heat and simmer
gently for about 45 minutes,
stirring the sauce occasionally.

Greek Cooking Essentials

Here are a few core
ingedients that are
always in my kitchen
and enable you to
complete a Greek
meal at any time.

CONDIMENTS

good-quality olive oil

red wine vinegar

white wine vinegar

caster sugar

icing sugar

salt

pepper

SPICES

dried oregano

mint (*diosmos*)

parsley

rosemary

cinnamon

cloves

allspice

nutmeg

chamomile

sage (*faskomilo*)

basil (*vasilikos*)

bay leaves (*daphne*)

cumin

coriander seeds

fennel seeds

aniseed

mahlepi

LEGUMES, GRAINS AND STARCHES

nuts

lentils, beans
and chickpeas

pasta

potatoes

rice
(for soups and pilaf)

plain flour

strong white flour

self-raising flour

CHEESES AND DAIRY PRODUCTS

feta

kasseri

kefalograviera

kefalotiri

mitzithra

milk

yoghurt

OTHER

tomatoes

onions

olives

lemons

eggs

sardines

vanilla

masticha

Important Greek Phrases

XRISTOS ANESTI	Christ has risen
XRONIA POLLA	(Used to wish a person happiness and a long prosperous life. Commonly used on feast days and Name Days.)
KALI OREXI	(Used when sitting at a table to wish everyone a pleasant and enjoyable meal. Similar to 'Bon Appetit'.)
KALA XRISTOUYENA	Merry Christmas
STIN EYIA SAS	To good health
ELATE STO TRAPEZI	Come to the table
YIA SOU	Hi
TI KANEIS	How are you?
KALIMERA	Good morning
KALISPERA	Good afternoon
KALINIHTA	Good night
SE AGAPO	I love you
AGAPI MOU	My love

Index

Index

Index

ACKNOWLEDGMENTS

This book is the result of a dream
that has become a reality thanks
to many people.

Firstly, I would like to thank
David Tenenbaum of Melbourne Books,
who believed in me and gave me a chance.

My friend Kathy Demos, who helped in so many
different ways. She was always there for me,
especially during challenging moments.

Tim Sutherland and Elise Lampe of Studio Brave,
who called this book their 'baby' and are
responsible for making it such a special book.

John Laurie for his brilliant photography,
and Leesa O'Reilly, who, as a stylist,
gave the dishes such beauty.

My sister-in-law, Katerina Angelopoulos,
and my mother-in-law, Anastasia Angelopoulos,
for all their help with the red eggs and
the Thiples.

A very special thank you to Alia Galatis,
who worked tirelessly, typing up all
the recipes.

To my mother, who taught me what I know and
has inspired me all my life. Her strength,
courage and determination are my inspiration,
and it is this strength that enabled me
to face my battle with cancer.

To my dad, who walks with me everywhere I go.

And last, but definitely not least, I thank
my husband, Peter, for his unconditional
love and support, and my two sons, Simon and
Jonathan Angelopoulos. They are all the
air that I breathe, my inspiration, and the
reason that I never gave up and never will.

Published by Melbourne Books
Level 9, 100 Collins Street,
Melbourne, VIC 3000
Australia
www.melbournebooks.com.au
info@melbournebooks.com.au

Copyright © 2013 Kathy Tsaples

Title: Sweet Greek™: Simple Food, Sumptuous Feasts
Author: Tsaples, Kathy
ISBN: 9781922129161 (hbk.)
Sixth printing: October 2022, Printed in China

A catalogue record for this
book is available from the
National Library of Australia

Designed by: Studio Brave
Photography: John Laurie
Food Stylist: Leesa O'Reilly

www.sweetgreek.com.au
Facebook & Instagram: @sweetgreekshop

Ὀδηγίαι. Δ...

12. Οὐγγίαι Ζάκχαρις
1η/ 150 δράμια Κόλλα
12 1/2 Οὐγγίαι Νερό
4. δράμια ξυνό

1ον θὰ δέσετε ἐωθα ἐμιον[
δὲς πρό, να θώσιν τη ζάνχ...
δη βράσιν θα θο ξαφρίσε...
διόλη δέ ἀμέσως μέσα θα...
... πρι διὰ να κοπη η βο...
... θι ξαφρίσει θα' οιξ...
... τῇ κοπη... 2 1/2...